# ROMAN ELEGIES
*and*
# THE DIARY

Johann Wolfgang von Goethe

# ROMAN ELEGIES

*and*

# THE DIARY

BILINGUAL EDITION

Verse translation by David Luke
Introduction by Hans Rudolf Vaget

Libris

1988

Translation, Postscript and Notes © David Luke, 1988
Introduction © Hans R. Vaget, 1988
This edition © Libris Ltd, 1988
*Roman Elegies II–XXIII* first published by Chatto & Windus 1977
This edition first published 1988

Libris, 10 Burghley Road, London NW5 1UE

ISBN 1-870352-05-X *(hardback)*
ISBN 1-870352-20-3 *(paperback)*

British Library Cataloguing in Publication Data:

Goethe, Johann Wolfgang von
Roman Elegies; and The Diary.——Bilingual ed.
I. Title   II. Luke, David   III. Goethe,
Johann Wolfgang von   IV. The Diary
V. Goethe, Johann Wolfgang von. Römische
Elegien. *English & German*
831'.6 PT1895.E7

Designed and produced by Cinamon and Kitzinger, London
Typeset by Wyvern Typesetting Limited, Bristol
Printed and bound in Great Britain by
Redwood Burn Limited, Trowbridge, Wiltshire

# CONTENTS

# PREFACE

Goethe's *Römische Elegien* have usually been printed as a cycle of twenty poems, a further four being excluded for reasons which are discussed in the Introduction. In the present edition they are presented as twenty-four, the excluded four elegies being restored to their proper places, in accordance with what appears to have been Goethe's original intention; the cycle is consequentially renumbered, the restored poems now being numbers I, III, XVII and XXIV. The text of the supposedly 'canonical' twenty is that of all the standard editions since Goethe's lifetime, including the historical-critical Weimar Edition (*WA*) which began appearing in 1887 (see note 34 to the Introduction); it is there printed in vol. 1, pp. 232–62. That of the offending four was suppressed in all the editions until the *WA*, and even there it was prudishly edited and relegated to an appendix of vol. 1, not appearing in full until vol. 53 (pp. 3–7), a late supplementary volume published in 1914.

*Das Tagebuch* was also long suppressed, as the Introduction explains, and there are textual problems in it which even the most modern editions do not quite resolve. We here use the version established by Hans Rudolf Vaget in his study *Goethe. Der Mann von 60 Jahren* (see Introduction, note 33). The translation of *Römische Elegien* (nos II–XXII) is a revised version of that previously published by Chatto & Windus (*Roman Elegies*, 1977), which did not include Elegies I and XXIV; that of *Das Tagebuch* appears here for the first time.

The Introduction is essentially the work of Hans Rudolf Vaget, with a few passages added in collaboration with David Luke. The material following the texts (Translator's Postscript and Explanatory Notes) is by David Luke, in consultation with Hans Rudolf Vaget.

D.L
H.R.V.

# INTRODUCTION

In a brief statement addressed, at the very end of his life, to the young poets of 1830, Goethe described himself as their 'liberator'.[1]* There is abundant evidence to justify this proud self-characterization by the octogenarian poet, and some of the most striking is to be found in his erotic poetry. At virtually every stage of his career, even when he seems to be engaged in purely restorative projects such as Weimar Classicism, Goethe's poetry was breaking new ground. Although he later repudiated, and in *Faust* ironized, the gospel of original genius, Goethe as a poet remained committed to innovation. This is especially true of those instances in which, seeming merely to pay tribute to tradition, he engaged with the canonical models of antiquity and transformed them, as he did in the *Roman Elegies*.

At the time when Goethe first made his mark on German and European literature, in the early 1770s, the ideal of originality, with its far-reaching implications, was asserting itself as the most seductive and powerful of the new currents of aesthetic thought that had entered the German-speaking territories from France and especially from England. Goethe's writings of his early Strasbourg and Frankfurt period, culminating in the tragic lyrical novel *The Sorrows of Young Werther* (1774), gave validity to the battle-cry for original genius and inspired the young generation's desire to be liberated from the norms of literary and social authority. Thus it was only natural that the group of 'Sturm und Drang' (Storm and Stress) writers, as they came to be known, looked to Goethe as their leader. Although this informal association was only a brief one, it left a more lasting imprint on his entire literary production than is generally realized. After his breakthrough in the early 1770s his poetry remained, as if by instinct, inimical to poetic convention. Goethe succeeded effortlessly, it seems, in finding his authentic voice.

To the casual observer, Goethe's youthful Storm and Stress period may appear a mere stepping-stone on the way to more mature tasks, or – to invoke one of his favourite images – a skin that had to be shed in the

* See notes on pp. 28ff.

1

course of what he saw as the organic growth of his personality. A more careful reader, however, will soon realize that Goethe's entire poetic production remained grounded in the aesthetic sensibility of his early breakthrough period. The best word to describe that sensibility might well be 'pan-erotic'. At the vital core of his creative personality, this most protean of poets remained faithful to 'young Werther', his early and perhaps most authentic self-projection, long after he had 'outgrown' the fever and ecstasy associated with that name. Late in his life, in 'An Werther' ('To Werther'), the opening poem of the famous Marienbad triptych (1823/4) which he called 'Trilogie der Leiden-schaft' ('Trilogy of Passion'), Goethe acknowledged as if with regret the subterranean continuity of that sensibility:

> Dann zog uns wieder ungewisse Bahn
> Der Leidenschaften labyrinthisch an.

> And then again, passion's uncertain maze
> Drew us into its labyrinthine ways.

We should not, however, attribute too much biographical truth to the lamenting voice of 'An Werther'. It appears that Goethe actually longed for the return of Werther and what he stood for. As he grew older, most clearly after the death of Schiller in 1805, Goethe engaged with increasing urgency in the project of recovering, through recollection and active remembrance, the creative energies of his youth. His autobiography, begun in 1809, represents only the most visible part of this enterprise. Goethe must have sensed that the more sophisticated and fragile poetic practices of his later years stood in need of the erotic energies that inform his early poetry. To the aging Goethe, 'renewed puberty' ('wiederholte Pubertät'), as he called it in a telling and much-quoted phrase,[2] had become a biological as well as a literary phantasm – but a phantasm of remarkable potency. It is in this context that a poem such as *The Diary*, which thematizes the creative force of remembering, acquires a significance beyond its more obvious narrative of erotic adventure.

From what did Goethe liberate German poetry? The brief essay in which he lays claim to the title of liberator does not tell us. He does not identify the fetters and conventions from which he had to free himself. Instead, he reminds his younger colleagues of the new freedom which poetry was now able to explore: the freedom to express the self. The young poets, he asserts, 'have through me become aware that, just as man must live from within, the artist must express his own self by revealing – no matter how he does it – only his own specific individuality'.[3] Simple and general though they may sound to us today, Goethe's parting words to his fellow poets make a basic point – a point that was crucial in the particular historical moment of his beginnings when both Goethe and German poetry were in their 'puberty': namely, that the poet's distinctive role is to express a world in his own authentic voice.

Goethe's statement of 1832 can be read not only as a piece of advice for young poets but, perhaps more productively, as a justification of his own poetic enterprise as a whole. No one before had put poetry so confidently at the service of self-expression and self-exploration. He had found himself at the threshold of an age that legitimized and encouraged the exploration of the self and gave it an entirely new sense of purpose. The Enlightenment had bequeathed to the Storm and Stress movement a new belief proclaiming the autonomy and wholeness of man. To the young Goethe, the source of this message was Johann Georg Hamann, the friend and teacher of his own mentor Herder. Goethe's autobiography, written some forty years later, still testifies eloquently to the liberating effect of Hamann's insistence on wholeness.[4] For Hamann, however, the self was an emphatically sexual being, and genius was to be defined as creativity in both the spiritual and the sexual sense. With characteristic bluntness Hamann declared in his *Socratic Memorabilia* (1759) that a genius without genitals is not a genius.

Goethe, whose concept of 'Humanität' owes much to Hamann, has contributed more to our awareness of the nature and force of desire than is generally realized, and more than any other poet in German literature. His work is surprisingly knowledgeable about androgyny, homoeroticism, incest, narcissism and fetishism. It is anything but an accident that Freud, a liberator on a different scale, turned to Goethe as one of his preferred case-studies, thus acknowledging him as a mythical precursor. It may well be argued, therefore, that to the extent that he relies on examples from the German literary imagination, 'Freud recognizes in Goethe the source and seed from which psychoanalysis was engendered' – with all the ambivalent dynamics that such paternity entails.[5]

Goethe's reputation as a poet of the erotic is well established. And yet, our knowledge of his erotic poetry in the precise sense rests on shaky foundations. The situation is nothing short of contradictory. On the one hand, generations of readers from the Romantics until today have admired the erotic freedom of his second novel, *Wilhelm Meister's Apprenticeship*, the elaborate apotheosis of Eros in *Faust*, and the spiritualized eroticism of *The West-Eastern Divan* which contains, arguably, the most sustained cycle of love-poems in the German language. On the other hand, however, there exists as yet no complete and universal appreciation of Goethe's explicitly sexual poetry, the poems that speak of 'true, naked love' – 'den echten, nacketen Amor' (Elegy III). To be sure, the *Roman Elegies* are now generally held in high esteem; most readers today would agree with E. M. Wilkinson's assessment of the *Elegies* as 'one of Goethe's finest works and a work unique in European literature'.[6] But Goethe's Roman cycle has never, until now, been presented to the general public in its entirety and in its original design. Most readers know it only in a truncated form. And Goethe's most daring and profound erotic poem, *The Diary*, is hardly known at all.

Whatever other conclusion we may draw from this paradox, it offers above all a clear object-lesson in the power of literary and social convention. That power is manifest, for instance, in Goethe's own diplomatic though reluctant self-censorship, and (with much less justification) in the long-standing refusal of Goethe scholars to admit *The Diary* and the suppressed parts of the *Roman Elegies* into the canon of his works. Beyond the obvious moral and social reasons for this stubborn misrepresentation, it is doubtless ultimately rooted in the innovative nature of Goethe's writing about the erotic. His poems in this genre, especially *The Diary*, mark such a bold break with the conventions of the older erotic poetry of the eighteenth century that for a long time, until recently in fact, they found only a few appreciative readers. Goethe's erotic poetry transcended what H. R. Jauss calls the 'horizon of expectation' in breaking with a powerful convention that had governed erotic poetry for centuries.[7] In Roman literature, erotic poetry dealt with the famous 'quinque lineae amoris', the five typical stages of erotic encounter: 'visus', 'allocutio', 'tactus', 'basium', 'coitus' – seeing, addressing, touching, kissing, and union.[8] Western love poetry since the Middle Ages and the Renaissance traditionally had to restrict itself to, at the most, four of the five classical stages. Writing explicitly of all five, as Goethe did in the *Roman Elegies* and *The Diary*, and writing about them in a serious rather than comic vein, constituted a violation of one of the strongest taboos of Western literature.

The extent to which the *Roman Elegies*, with their full-bodied celebration of sexual love, and *The Diary*, with its seemingly antithetical theme of sexual failure, are in fact linked has never been clearly recognized. What unites these two major texts is the ambition to create a new type of erotic poetry – poems set in the contemporary world and informed by an authentically modern sensibility. For the first essay in this genre, inevitably, the great Roman models had to serve as point of departure. In post-Classical, Christian Europe, the only way for poetry to explore the vast territory beyond the boundaries of convention was by mimicking the ancients and by borrowing their gestures and inflections. Thus Goethe turned quite consciously, and self-consciously, to the famous 'triumvirate' of Catullus, Tibullus, and Propertius (cf. Elegy VII). By reviving their canonical *erotica* in his own *Erotica Romana*, as the *Elegies* were first entitled, he placed himself under the protection, as it were, of their unassailable literary authority. But donning a classicist's cloak was as much a matter of poetic strategy as it was of prudence. It endowed these modern elegies with a rich intertextual resonance and thereby lifted them beyond the reach of the kind of biographical curiosity that had plagued Goethe ever since *Werther* (cf. Elegy IV).

Two decades later he turned to an even greater challenge in order to complete his project of a new erotic poetry. He now set the same kind of uninhibited, explicit, and serious *erotica* that he had realized so happily in the *Elegies* in the contemporary world of 1800 – complete with business trip, hotel, erotic encounter on the road, and loving wife at home. And, more fully than in the *Elegies*, he immersed this kind of writing about sexuality in an unmistakably contemporary bourgeois sensibility that wavers uneasily between obligation and passion – 'Pflicht' and 'Liebe' – the two pivotal concepts in the official legal and religious discourse on sexuality.

The new erotic poetry Goethe aimed at was to be different from the poems and verse novellas in this genre by his contemporaries Christoph Martin Wieland and Wilhelm Heinse; it was also to mark a complete break with his own early poetry written in the French Rococo style of the period with its languishing and teasing and its general air of inauthenticity. But Goethe's project, if we are to believe the experts, was doomed to be thwarted. Heinz Schlaffer, in his authoritative *Musa iocosa* (1971), has traced the history of erotic poetry in Germany to about 1770. The poetry written thereafter, in other words after the emergence of a distinct middle class in Germany, is dismissed as unrepresentative of middle-class morality, or as derivative from classical models. Erotic poetry, Schlaffer argues, proposes a lifestyle devoted to pleasure; it revolves round the promiscuity of independent persons without the restrictions of family ties. He therefore sees it as an essentially aristocratic genre, and as such incompatible with middle-class sensibility with its emphasis on the work ethic, family, and Christian morality.[9] How does *The Diary* fit into this scheme? Astonishingly, Schlaffer simply ignores it. One can see why. Here is a major text which, according to his neo-Marxist framework, should not exist: a modern erotic poem in a bourgeois setting, written independently of classical models and in open defiance of Christian morality.[10]

Goethe was of course quite conscious of the problems he faced as a modern erotic poet, and in a revealing and much-quoted conversation of 1824 with his secretarial protégé Johann Peter Eckermann, he commented on some of them. He had given Eckermann two unpublished poems to read, one of which was *The Diary*. It must have been Goethe's intention on that obviously premeditated occasion to make some general observations – for the record, so to speak – on the power of convention and the detrimental influence it exerted on poetry. Eckermann played the part prescribed to him to the letter: he assured the poet that *The Diary*, at heart, was a perfectly moral work. He had to acknowledge, however, that the public could not but regard it as immoral on account of its 'naturalism' and forthrightness. Goethe agreed, observing that poets are forced by the conventions of the day to keep some of their best writing to themselves, and blaming this on the public's lack of true civilization – of 'intellect and superior culture' ('Geist und höhere Bildung'). But, he remarked, times change, and there may soon be a time in which poets can speak again with greater freedom. For time is

a whimsical tyrant, which in every century has a different face for all one says and does. We can no longer say with propriety things that were permitted to

6

the ancient Greeks; and the Englishman of 1820 cannot endure what suited the vigorous contemporaries of Shakespeare, so that at the present day it is found necessary to have a Family Shakespeare.[11]

It is sad to see how countless self-appointed guardians of Goethe's reputation, by bowing to the whimsical tyrant Convention, have fashioned for generations of readers just such a 'Family Goethe'.

The *Roman Elegies*, though written in Weimar, belong essentially to Goethe's Italian period (September 1786 – April 1788), specifically his second Roman sojourn of the first four months of 1788. As with the *Duino Elegies* of Rainer Maria Rilke, their title refers primarily to the locale in which they were conceived.[12] Goethe's *Elegies* are in spirit inseparable from his Italian sojourn, which marks a turning-point in his life. In 1786 he was thirty-seven, and it was eleven years since he had established himself at the small ducal court of Weimar, where he had been beset by various responsibilities of public office, by tensions in his increasingly problematical relationship with Charlotte von Stein, and last but not least by a growing sense of frustration in his poetic endeavours. Suddenly, relying on the understanding friendship of his patron the Duke Karl August, he took unofficial leave and fled to the south.

What made this journey a central event in Goethe's life? In most accounts, including Goethe's own (written much later), we read chiefly of his observations of the Italian landscape, his scientific speculations, his delight in paintings and architecture, his joy in being at last on the 'classical soil' (Elegy VII) for which he had so long craved, his general sense of rejuvenation, indeed of rebirth, as an artist. But we may well guess that the real, if less publicized, heart of the matter was something more intimate and elemental. It was in Rome, apparently, that Goethe experienced a personal sexual liberation, which proved all the more powerful in that it was in all likelihood his first successful sexual relationship. It has, indeed, been suggested that until then he had suffered from a sexual disorder (*ejaculatio praecox*) which rendered him incapable of achieving intercourse.[13]

Naturally, in view of such weighty biographical matters, there has been a good deal of curiosity and speculation about the identity of Goethe's Roman mistress. From scattered hints we can gather that she was a young widow (see Elegy VIII) who accepted the well-defined role

7

of the *mantenuta* – the kept woman. It would obviously be wrong, however, merely to read Goethe's poems as a faithful representation of his relationship with that shadowy Roman figure. For the lovers' idyll in the *Roman Elegies* is clearly a literary construct firmly anchored in mythology and in the poetry of his chosen precursors. Or take the name of the poet's beloved, 'Faustina' – a name that marks her as the fictitious partner of an equally fictitious Faust. Ironically, Goethe was working on *Faust* at that very time; in fact, he wrote some of its most characteristically 'northern' scenes in Rome. Was even the invention of the name 'Faustina' perhaps an ironic recognition of his own 'Faustian' longings? After all, the Roman experience had in some sense satisfied an essential part of them – Faust's desire to 'embrace infinite Nature', to suck at the very breasts of mother earth, as the earliest version of the text puts the matter, and his ambition to win the 'crown of humanity'.[14] In any event, it is plain that the transformation of biographical matter, such as it is, was controlled by a pervasive ironic self-consciousness, by playfulness, and last but not least by more than a trace of narcissism.

As if to emphasize specifically the distance between poetry and biographical truth, Goethe later made the following comment on the public's apparently irrepressible curiosity about the 'facts' behind his *Roman Elegies*: 'People seldom reflect that a poet can generally make something good out of very little.'[15]

Shortly after his return to Weimar, Goethe met Christiane Vulpius. She was twenty-three, unmarried, and employed in a local manufactory of artificial flowers. Her brother Christian August Vulpius, a then impoverished writer, had asked her to present a petition to Goethe on his behalf; she did so in July 1788 as he was walking in the park outside his small villa by the river Ilm in Weimar. Christiane lived with Goethe as his mistress until 1806, then as his wife until her death in 1816. They had five children (1789, 1791, 1793, 1795, 1802) of whom only the first, August, survived infancy. All Weimar was scandalized by this open liaison with a poorly educated young woman, who when company came would address Goethe formally as 'Herr Privy Councillor' and tactfully disappear. Especially offended was Frau von Stein, the married lady with whom since his arrival in Weimar Goethe had maintained a passionate but, it seems, wholly platonic relationship. When his new arrangements became known, this friendship suffered an irreparable breach. But the relationship with Christiane, whom he called his 'little nature-creature' ('kleines Naturwesen'), was lasting and, so far as we know, entirely faithful.[16] Initially she had simply taken over the role of the Roman 'Faustina'. Goethe was obviously determined to keep alive his newly-found source of strength and inspiration. Would he also be able to transfer to the northern world with its gloomy skies and hostile moral climate the kind of poetry he had envisioned under the southern ether?

It is interesting to see the direction his poetry first took. In 'The Visit' ('Der Besuch') and 'Lament at Dawn' ('Morgenklagen')', two long-ish poems written in August 1788, Goethe painted two scenes of dis-creet, domestic eroticism. These otherwise unremarkable texts allow us to see clearly the dilemma confronting Goethe – or indeed any other poet at that time – with respect to erotic subjects. The choice was between contemporary form with conventional subject matter, and daring subject matter in classical form. What was not permissible, it seems, was to be daring in an authentically modern idiom. Goethe therefore opted at this point for a poetic form (five-beat trochaic lines, and unrhymed stanzas of irregular length) which sounded contemporary but which allowed no more than a restrained and conventional suggestion of sexuality.

Goethe took an altogether different route in his *Roman Elegies*, which he began writing in October 1788, shortly after he began to live with Christiane. This route was to lead him immeasurably further in his project of creating a modern erotic poetry than the two texts written in August of that year. If poetry was to speak of sexuality with the same honesty and depth as had been achieved in other realms of human experience, it had to disguise its voice. Already in 'The Visit' Goethe had taken up a classical motif from Propertius (that of the lover's contemplation of the sleeping beloved; cf. also Elegy XV). Now Propertius and, to a lesser extent, Tibullus and Catullus were to provide an intertextual matrix that could sustain and legitimize the naturalness and frankness Goethe was aiming at. By the same token, poetic speech also had to accommodate itself to the patterns and accents of the precursors. The *Roman Elegies* are founded on the realization that in modern times erotic poetry depended on classical form for its very survival. The elegiac distich that Goethe chose to adopt for this purpose proved, on the whole, effective enough in achieving the subtle distancing that was essential to the success of the under-taking.

Goethe must have intended to publish his *Elegies* soon after their completion in 1790. One of them (Elegy XV) appeared in a periodical in 1791. He was apparently contemplating publishing more, if not all of them, when he was advised against doing so by Karl August, as well as by Herder, the friend and mentor of his Storm and Stress days who was now an important church dignitary in Weimar. Goethe took their advice 'blindly', as he wrote, somewhat resentfully, to his close friend Karl Ludwig von Knebel,[17] and the *Elegies* were suppressed for several years. This of course appeared to imply a quite mistaken categorization of them as that kind of pornographic literary exercise which had to remain private. But the *Elegies* finally did appear in 1795, in Schiller's journal *Die Horen*.

Schiller's role in the literary fortunes of the *Elegies* turned out to be a crucial one. As with *Wilhelm Meister's Apprenticeship*, the traditional misreading of which as the classic idealistic *Bildungsroman* (novel of self-cultivation) was initiated by Schiller, his reading of the *Roman Elegies*, too, left a lasting imprint on later generations of readers. Schiller was impressed by the poems, but one cannot overlook the fact that their 'liberty in the portrayal of Nature' caused him a certain amount of embarrassment. On first hearing the *Elegies* read to him by the author, he characterized them in a letter to his wife as '*risqué*, to be sure, and not very decent' ('zwar schlüpfrig und nicht sehr dezent') but added that they belonged among the best of Goethe's works.[18] In 1795, in a letter to his patron the Duke of Schleswig-Holstein-Augusten-burg, he defended their publication on the grounds of their 'lofty poetic beauty', adding that in his view 'they offend against a certain conventional decency, but not against that decency which is true and natural' ('die wahre und natürliche Dezenz').[19] This question of 'Dezenz' clearly troubled him; he therefore resolved to clarify the whole problem in a 'brief essay', 'On the Modesty of Poets' ('Über die Schamhaftigkeit der Dichter'). But instead of writing such an essay, he incorporated his thoughts on the matter into the famous treatise *On Naive and Sentimental Poetry* (*Über naive und sentimentalische Dichtung*) (1797), Schiller's influential typological study of classical and modern literature. In that text, Schiller offers a generous appreciation and defence of Goethe's *Elegies* – but at a price.

Schiller clearly has the *Roman Elegies* in mind when he draws a distinction between the kind of erotic poetry that is 'objectionable' and 'vulgar' and a kind that is beautiful and noble. He argues forcefully that whenever the poet merely intends to titillate our desires, his work becomes empty, cold, and 'without exception objectionable' ('verwerflich'). But he will produce something 'beautiful, noble, and praiseworthy, in defiance of all frosty decency', if he can combine sophistication and emotion (literally 'mind and heart', 'Geist und Herz'), and if his writing is 'naive'.[20] Herein lies the crux. The term 'naive' in the Schillerian sense denotes 'in the spirit and manner of the ancients'. Schiller employs the term to differentiate between the essentially reflective, self-conscious manner of post-classical, modern literature, and the classical, essentially straightforward manner of the Greeks. It is difficult for us today to comprehend why Schiller would classify Goethe in general and the *Roman Elegies* in particular as examples of 'naive' poetry. Goethe's poems are so obviously grounded in an awareness of his own historical distance from his Latin models that we may well wonder why Schiller chose this particular critical strategy. We may well speculate that he needed to set off his own, more philosophically inclined writing against Goethe's and thus justify it as different from, but of equal value to, the idealized model of poetic 'naivety'.

Again, as in the case of *Wilhelm Meister's Apprenticeship*, Schiller's highly sophisticated reading of the *Roman Elegies* must, in the last analysis, be termed a misreading. Given Schiller's status in Goethe criticism generally, his characterization of Goethe's poems had far-reaching consequences. Perhaps its most problematic effect may be seen in the persistent tendency, especially in German criticism, to set Goethe somewhat apart from the mainstream of European Romanticism. This critical topos is largely responsible for the failure to recognize the thoroughly modern and innovative mode of the *Roman Elegies*. It has also led to a failure to recognize the innovative tendency of Weimar Classicism in its imaginative endeavours as distinct from its aesthetic theories – a tendency of which Goethe's *Elegies* stand as the most representative example.

Most editions of Goethe's works present the *Elegies* as a twenty-part cycle. This is the arrangement in which they were first published in

1795 under the title *Elegien. Rom, 1788*. There is considerable evidence, however, that this familiar arrangement, which Goethe authorized for posterity in the final edition of his works, owes its order more to the dictates of convention and to self-censorship than to artistic considerations, as some commentators have tried to argue. It is important to know that Goethe had submitted to Schiller not twenty but twenty-two elegies for publication in *Die Horen*. After some discussion, he agreed to excise two of them altogether rather than publish them in fragmentary form, with lines omitted, as Schiller had suggested. It is not entirely clear whether it was Goethe or Schiller who first considered dropping the two elegies. Given Schiller's initial ambivalence about their immodesty, we may assume that it was he who felt prompted to urge caution. In any case, he reported to his friend Körner: 'The coarsest of Goethe's *Elegies* have been omitted, in order not to offend too much against decency.'[21] We may also assume that Goethe consented out of concern for the well-being of the fledgling journal and tact towards Schiller, who had only recently become his friend and ally.

The two excised elegies appear harmless enough and will hardly strike anyone today as offensive. In the first of them (no. III in the present edition) the splendour of Roman palaces is contrasted with the simplicity of the beloved's room. The poem concludes with a wonderfully resonant evocation of the pleasures of sexual union:

Ours is the true, the authentic, the naked Love; and beneath us,
    Rocking in rhythm, the bed creaks the dear song of our joy.

The reasons for suppressing the other elegy (XVII) seem a little more persuasive. It speaks of the universally dreaded danger of contracting venereal disease not only from a prostitute but also – and this seems to have been the real stumbling-block – from one's own wife:

Who does not hesitate now to break faith with a tedious mistress?
    Love may not hold us, but sheer caution will make us think twice.
Even at home, who knows! Not a single pleasure is risk-free;
    Who in his own wife's lap now lays a confident head?
Neither in wedlock now nor out of it can we be certain;
    Mutually noxious we are, husband and lover and wife.

To readers of the nineteen eighties, dreading another 'new monster', these words may seem more prophetic than even Goethe can have suspected.

But even if these two elegies were restored to their proper place in the cycle, as they are in some editions, we could still not claim to know the *Roman Elegies* in their entirety and in the order in which Goethe conceived them. Originally, the *Erotica Romana* were to include two more elegies, making twenty-four in all. Both are celebrations of the phallic fertility-god Priapus, and for this reason Goethe did not even bother to submit them to Schiller. The earthiness and frankness traditionally associated with poetry in the Priapean vein obviously disqualified them from publication. This, however, should not obscure the fact that they represent a crucial part of Goethe's project as a whole.

Goethe was reading at that time not only the erotic poetry of the classical 'triumvirate' but also the far less respectable *Carmina Priapea*. These were a collection, or perhaps cycle, of about eighty epigrammatic poems in honour of Priapus, dating from the first century A D.[22] They had enjoyed a certain underground currency throughout the centuries, especially among the sixteenth-century Humanists. It is clear that Goethe had more than a nodding acquaintance with these poems. He studied them in the winter of 1789/90 in a seventeenth-century edition furnished with learned commentaries by Renaissance scholars,[23] and wrote his own learned comments on nine of the poems, emulating his predecessors by proposing textual emendations. His commentary – in Latin, of course – was addressed to 'Princeps Augustus', which probably refers to the Duke Karl August of Weimar, who savoured such writings and was a frequent recipient of Goethe's sexual confidences.[24] Analysing Goethe's essay on the *Priapea*, Kurt Eissler rightly observes that it

explores topics of intense emotional value. Under the guise of philology the forbidden and the obscene are brought to light and made the subject of communication. This combination of dry objectivity with the indecent makes the charm of these seemingly casual compositions. Psychologically, however, they are not as casual as their author wishes to make it appear [ . . . ] He was fascinated by the subject like someone who has started to fathom its full meaning and now cannot wrest his mind from his interest in it.[25]

This personal, biographical motif notwithstanding, Goethe's reading of the *Priapea* must be viewed as part of his work on the *Elegies*. He himself explained as much in his introductory remarks to the Duke:

It is not vouchsafed to man, as it is to the sparrows, to enjoy Venus continually, and many men join with Schoppe in deploring this circumstance. But I have always, most excellent Prince, been of a mind not anxiously to yearn for what chance has denied me, and accordingly I have always endeavoured to fill out with some useful or agreeable occupation the intervals by which Nature has separated my pleasures. On the same principle I have also been amusing myself, in the long nights of this winter which is now drawing to a close, by passing them alternately with Venus and with the more indulgent Muses.[26]

The pages on some of the *Priapea* which he enclosed with these remarks were meant to testify to the more pleasurable of his nocturnal activities.

Reading and writing erotic poetry had indeed become more pleasurable to Goethe that winter. It was the time of Christiane's first pregnancy. On 25 December 1789 she gave birth to August, only survivor of their five children. Goethe's reference to the 'more indulgent Muses' clearly implies some creative work – not just his reading of the *Priapea* but his writing of *erotica* in general. Quite obviously he presents his interest in Priapean poetry as part of his work on the *Roman Elegies*, and Goethe's own Priapean elegies should therefore be considered an inseparable part of the larger project.

One cannot help feeling somewhat baffled by the strange configuration of interests that dominated Goethe's thoughts in the winter of 1789–1790. Shortly after the outbreak of the Revolution in France, which he observed with the greatest apprehension and which turned into *the* political trauma of his life, he devoted a great deal of time to what appears to be an entirely unconnected activity: the creation of a poetry born from a most private 'revolution' in his own sexual life. Or is there a hidden connection?

Without wishing to press the matter unduly, one is in fact tempted to see a parallel, however sketchy, between the radicalism of the events unfolding in France and the radicalism of Goethe's attempt to liberate German poetry from the tyranny of certain conventions. In the light of this correspondence, his preoccupation with Priapus and Priapean poetry assumes a new significance beyond the obviously psychological one. The ancient deity of fertility, traditionally depicted with an outsize wooden penis, represented the low, popular strata of the culture of antiquity.[27] This is true of the early Greek monuments documenting the cult of Priapus and of the Roman *Priapea* of the first century A D, which represent a late, parodistic stage of the cult. Goethe clearly wanted to reach back to these popular and coarser elements of erotic poetry. Did he believe that the creation of truly liberated poetry was predicated on recovering the phallic deity? Or was he guided by an intuitive understanding of the central role of the phallus in human sexuality – thereby anticipating a central aspect of Freud? We can't be sure. What we can say with certainty is that the resurrection of Priapus epitomizes the decidedly anti-Christian emphasis of the *Roman Elegies*.

The official, technical term for the activity celebrated in Goethe's poems is fornication – a serious sin. In the language of the Church, all sexual gratification outside marriage was sinful; and even in marriage, the limits of sex were carefully circumscribed in view of the divine injunction to procreate. But as Michel Foucault has shown, it was precisely the official stance of the Church with its highly knowledgeable and sophisticated discourse on sexuality, dating from the early Church Fathers, that paradoxically spurred and deepened the awareness of sexuality.[28] The moral teachings of the Christian churches by no means eliminated the need for erotic poetry. They helped rather to sharpen the focus. This is less evident in the *Roman Elegies*, with its two unmarried lovers, than it is in *The Diary*, where by choosing a married protagonist Goethe focused more clearly on the fundamental Christian concepts governing sexual activity.

In the first of Goethe's Priapean poems, the poet develops a stock motif of the *Priapea* and appoints Priapus as the guardian of his own 'garden', which here of course stands for the *Elegies* themselves. Anyone is welcome to help himself to the golden fruit of life that grows here: Priapus is also instructed to punish with his mighty instrument all 'miscreants', who may come to defile the garden and all 'hypocrites' who would express disgust at the 'fruits of pure nature'. This short poem has an unmistakable introductory function.

In the other, somewhat longer poem, Priapus himself speaks: he gives thanks to the 'honest' poet for having rescued him from neglect and abuse and for having restored him to his rightful place among the gods – a vindication accomplished through the *Roman Elegies*. As a reward Priapus promises the poet the joys of fabulous sexual potency:

> Therefore I bless your magnificent central rod, may it always
>     Stand up half a foot tall at your beloved's behest.
> May your member not tire, until you have both done the dozen
>     Figures Philaenis describes, finished the dance of your joy.

It is not difficult to see the structural function of these two Priapean elegies: they are clearly meant to form a frame for the other twenty-two.[29] Such a framing device is quite in keeping with the structure of the *Carmina Priapea* which, as Vinzenz Buchheit has shown, display several such framings.[30] In the opening poem of the *Roman Elegies*, the 'prologue', where one would traditionally expect an invocation of the Muses or of Venus, Goethe calls instead upon Priapus as the true genius of the poetry that is to follow. And the other Priapean elegy, the 'epilogue', reveals and confirms the secret mission of the *Elegies*: the recovery and vindication of Priapus.

It may be recalled here that the theme of recovery – of rehabilitation or 'Rettung' – is fundamental to Goethe's literary identity. Many of his early literary projects were undertaken with the express intent of recovering a historical or mythical figure from neglect or opprobrium. This applies for instance to the historical drama *Götz von Berlichingen* (1771), to the narrative poem 'Hans Sachs's Poetic Mission' (1776), and above all to *Faust* (begun in the early 1770s) which carries the idea of 'Rettung' (literally 'saving') to its most far-reaching implications. In the *Roman Elegies*, this fundamental gesture of recovery is focused on Priapus. And as in the other cases, the recovery of the deposed and abused phallic god may be viewed as an act of liberation – liberation, that is, from outdated and unproductive paradigms of erotic poetry.

It will now be obvious that our reading of the *Roman Elegies* must be significantly affected once we have accepted the Priapean frame as an integral part of the cycle. The two Priapean texts reinforce the importance of the allusion in Elegy XIII, at the centre of the cycle, to the phallic god, the 'glorious son' of Dionysos and Aphrodite. Furthermore, they allow us to identify the 'genius' invoked at the beginning of Elegy II as Priapus. He, and not some vague *genius loci* as most commentators think, is the true genius of the *Roman Elegies*. Instead of centring the cycle's poetic aim on some vaguely felt interplay of present and past, or of 'ROMA' and 'AMOR', we can now define it more confidently and precisely as the recovery of Priapus, who is present, explicitly and implicitly, in the *Elegies* as a whole. Finally, the Priapean frame alerts the reader from the outset to the basically ironic posture of a work that playfully mediates between the paganism of the fiction and the entirely Christian consciousness of the implied reader. This irony is often overlooked and with it what may be considered the most distinctive and innovative feature of Goethe's erotic poetry: its self-conscious reflection on the dilemma of the modern erotic poet. This self-consciousness forms perhaps the most aesthetically satisfying aspect of the *Roman Elegies*; it surfaces even more powerfully twenty years later in the other major work of Goethe's erotic poetry, *The Diary*.

The publication history of *The Diary* is even more curious than that of the *Elegies*.[31] Again we have a case of self-censorship by Goethe. He wrote *The Diary*, or finished it, in April 1810, and all the evidence suggests that he regarded it as a poem of some importance, but one which it would be impossible to publish. He thus consigned it, with other 'impossible' texts such as the Satanic Mass intended for the 'Walpurgis Night' section in *Faust*, to what he called his 'Walpurgis sack'.[32] He did, however, enjoy reading it aloud or showing it to various friends. Only two manuscripts of the poem appear to have survived: one in the hand of Friedrich Wilhelm Riemer (Goethe's resident philological adviser and the private tutor of his son August) with a few emendations in Goethe's own hand, and another copy by someone unknown.[33] An original autograph seems to have existed but it has never been found. *The Diary* was first published in 1861, in a privately printed, limited edition, by the Berlin bookdealer Salomon Hirzel, but just how the text of the poem found its way into the hands of Hirzel is not entirely clear. This first printing, based on what Hirzel believed to be Goethe's autograph, was the beginning of a whole series of under-the-counter special editions in which the poem regularly surfaced from its literary limbo for the next century or so. As was perhaps to be expected, the text has usually been read simply as a thinly veiled and altogether embarrassing confession by the sixty-year-old Goethe of an extramarital encounter thwarted by impotence.

In 1885, when the great 'Weimar Edition' of Goethe's works was in preparation under the patronage of Karl August's granddaughter-in-law the Grand Duchess Sophia,[34] its editors submitted the contents of the 'Walpurgis sack' to the patroness. Her Royal Highness, we are told, spent an evening with her ladies-in-waiting reading *The Diary* and the unpublished *Venetian Epigrams* aloud, and scratching words out with penknives; most have since been restored. She then decreed that all this material should continue to be withheld from publication. It was not until 1910, thirteen years after the Grand Duchess's death, that prudery was so far overcome by scholarly scruple as to permit the editors to include Hirzel's (corrupt) text of the poem in an obscure supplementary volume, hidden away among the critical apparatus.[35] But even here, the two most daring and notorious lines in the poem (135f.) were partly deleted and were not restored until 1914, buried even more obscurely in a list of variant readings.[36] Since then, the correct or nearly correct text has been properly included in the best complete editions of Goethe's works, but the whole poem is shunned in almost all anthologies, and even large scholarly multi-volume selections (such as the commonly used 'Hamburg Edition' by Erich Trunz) refrain from including *The Diary*. Special private printings of the poem on its own, however, continue unabated to this day, often furnished with frivolous and misleading illustrations. The first English translation (in prose) appeared in David Luke's bilingual selection of Goethe's verse (Penguin, 1964); the first English verse rendering was attempted by John Frederick Nims and published in 1968 in *Playboy Magazine*.

*The Diary* unfolds a carefully organized narrative that centres on the failure of an older man in a sexual encounter with a young woman. Poets have only rarely turned to this subject matter, and when they did the intent was, by and large, to ridicule the whole episode. Three notable examples of the motif may be found in Ovid's *Amores* (III 7), in Ariosto's *Orlando Furioso* (VIII 46ff.), and in *The Imperfect Enjoyment*, a poem by John Wilmot, Earl of Rochester.[37] Goethe seems not to have known Rochester's poem, but he was familiar with Ariosto's work from his youth and knew, of course, Ovid. But although both texts treat the same motif of sexual failure, the situation is in both cases quite different from that in Goethe's poem. In Ovid, the failure befalls a young man, and his partner – an older, more experienced woman – pretends to have succeeded in having intercourse all the same in order to avoid being teased by her female friends. The protagonist in Ariosto's episode is a lecherous old hermit who attempts to rape the sleeping

Angelica. There are some faint echoes of these two earlier examples in Goethe's poem, but they play no significant part in it.

A much more likely and fruitful point of departure was provided by his own *Roman Elegies*. There, in the concluding Priapean elegy, the poet was promised unfailing sexual potency as a reward for the labour of love by which he had restored Priapus. Here the same poet, disguised only thinly as a diary-writing travelling merchant, reflects explicitly on the inexplicable failure of his supposedly fail-safe gift from Priapus. In view of this, Goethe could conceivably have been prompted to revoke the recovery of Priapus accomplished in the *Elegies*. But the poem proposes nothing of the sort.

Further connections between the two texts can easily be detected. Like the *Elegies* in their original design, *The Diary* exhibits a twenty-four-part structure. The later poem also employs a framing device similar to that of the *Elegies*, and its structure displays an equally pronounced symmetry. Goethe obviously knew Eros well enough to realize that its natural lawlessness called for the discipline of form and the imposition of fairly rigid aesthetic laws. In both works, Goethe uses the same constellation of figures – a travelling writer and a young woman – thereby setting the stage for the central concern of both texts, though more explicitly of *The Diary*: namely, to reflect on the intimate interdependence of the act of love and the act of writing as two exemplary manifestations of human creativity. In the *Roman Elegies* (VII) this theme was immortalized in the motif of the poet tapping the rhythm of the hexameter on his beloved's back:

> Often I even compose my poetry in her embraces,
>> Counting hexameter beats, tapping them out on her back
> Softly, with one hand's fingers . . .

Goethe explores the relationship of writing to the love-act more confidently in *The Diary* by focusing on the failure of both sexual and artistic powers – the one mirroring and illuminating the other.

*The Diary* reflects with great clarity a particular dilemma in which the modern poet finds himself: the absence of an established canon of poetic forms adequate to the needs of erotic poetry. In the important conversation of February 1824 already cited, Goethe and Eckermann went on to discuss the 'mysterious and great effects produced by the different poetical forms'. Goethe observed that the *Roman Elegies*, had they been written 'in the style and metre of Byron's *Don Juan*', would be found 'quite infamous'. By the same token Eckermann would have preferred to see *The Diary* written in a classical metre. This, he felt, would have distanced it from contemporary reality. As it stood, the form of the poem did not provide the necessary veil of modesty for it to be allowed out into decent society. Clearly, it was not the subject matter of the poem but its form that troubled Eckermann. He was especially troubled by the fact that *The Diary* treated an erotic adventure 'of our day in the language of our day'.[38] But does the poem in fact employ the poetic idiom of 1810? There is no simple answer to this question. The vocabulary is unmistakably contemporary, hardly distinguishable from that of Goethe's novel *Die Wahlverwandtschaften* (*Elective Affinities*) (1809), its immediate neighbour chronologically. The use of *ottava rima*, on the other hand, does seem to hark back to an older poetic mode. What exactly is the function of this particular stanza form? And why would Goethe choose for *The Diary* the very form that would have made his *Roman Elegies* sound 'infamous'?

*Don Juan* could not, of course, be the model for the poetic form of Goethe's poem since it antedates Byron's work by some ten years. Rather, they both look back to the same great model of all modern writing in *ottava rima*, the *Orlando Furioso* of 'Meister Ariost' as Eckermann calls him. And this throws into relief a basic dilemma of modern poetry: the disparity between the contemporary experience of the erotic and the historical modes of erotic writing on which the poet, for lack of a continuous tradition, is obliged to rely. In *The Diary*, such a disparity can clearly be felt between the thoroughly contemporary flavour of the erotic adventure and the historical garb in which it is clad, between the 'naturalism' of the theme and the stateliness and elaborate splendour of its form.

Given the rather rigid technical requirements of *ottava rima*, it is not surprising that Goethe used it only sparingly and on special occasions. It is therefore all the more instructive to note for what kind of text he did use it. One immediately thinks of 'Orphic Primal Words' ('Urworte. Orphisch') (1817) with its profound reflections on individual destiny, chance, love, necessity and hope – each theme concentrated into the eight lines of a single stanza; or of the moving commemorative poem about Schiller, 'Epilogue to Schiller's *Song of the Bell*' ('Epilog zu Schillers *Glocke*') (1805). Other examples are

'The Mysteries' ('Die Geheimnisse'), a puzzling, symbolic epic begun
in 1784 but which remained a fragment, and especially the two poems
called 'Dedication' ('Zueignung'): the first (1784) originally intended
as a prologue to 'The Mysteries' and one of Goethe's great
self-assessments as a poet, and the other (1797) also reflecting on his
life and poetic career at the time of resuming the composition of *Faust*
and standing as a 'dedicatory' prologue to his *opus magnum*. The
company of such personal and esoteric poems provides a somewhat
surprising but illuminating context for *The Diary*. It seems to indicate
that this poem, too, speaks of something mysterious and profound, as
do all his other texts in this particular form.

We know that, apart from Ariosto, Goethe had another, more recent
Italian model in mind: the enormously successful *Novelle galanti in
Ottaverime* by the Abbate Giambattista Casti. Goethe had made the
acquaintance of this clerical author in Rome, where he heard him recite
one of his verse novellas, *L'Arcivescovo di Praga*. Goethe found it
'slightly improper, but extraordinarily well written in *ottava rima*'.[39]
Not surprisingly, he refreshed his memory of Casti's writing when he
himself, in August 1808, contemplated a not so respectable subject-
matter for a *novella galante* of sorts. It appears that the idea for *The
Diary* first occurred to him during the early stages of his work on
*Elective Affinities*. He returned to it after the completion of the novel
and actually wrote the poem in 1810. This suggests that the idea of *The
Diary* was in his mind during the whole of the intense period in which
he composed *Elective Affinities*. A startling configuration indeed,
especially in view of the thematic affinities between the two works![40]
The novel as well as the poem are about marriage and about an adultery
which both happens and does not happen, and at the centre of both
works we find a psychological situation in which the libido is aroused
by an absent object of desire rather than by the present partner. But the
two texts stand at opposite poles in their manner of resolving this
situation: in the novel its consequences are inexorably tragic, whereas
*The Diary*, as we shall see, proposes a conciliatory resolution. The
poem may thus be viewed as a corrective after-thought, as it were, with
which Goethe sought to restore the balance that had been upset by the
tragic force of the novel.

Casti's novellas treat erotic anecdotes in conventionally veiled form
and provide the reader with a rather predictable moral. In *The Diary*

Goethe appears to be toying with this convention of the genre. He places in the foreground the kind of erotic adventure one would expect to find in a *novella galante*, and he does offer a rather comforting moral. Or so its seems. But can we be sure that the poem in fact offers precisely the kind of moral the reader has been led to expect?

A married man of mature years, returning from a business trip, is forced to spend an additional night on the road because of a broken carriage-wheel. He is a writer of sorts who is in the habit, when absent from his wife, of recording his day's doings every night in a diary which he keeps for their mutual pleasure. At the inn he encounters an irresistibly attractive servant-girl. That night, inexplicably, he is quite unable to write the usual fluent entries in his diary. It turns out that he is also incapable of making love to the girl who has joined him in his room, desirous of making him her first lover. Thrown into despair by his unexpected impotence, and lying awake next to the girl, he begins to recall in loving detail the untroubled pleasures of making love in his youth with the young woman who became and still is his wife. He remembers with particular vividness their wedding and the wedding ceremony – and this sets the stage for one of the most provocative gestures in all of Goethe, the confrontation of the crucifix and the erect male sexual organ:

> And when at last we wed, I do confess,
> Before that altar and that priest, before
> Thy wretched bloodstained cross, *domine Christe*,
> God pardon me! it stirred and rose, my *iste*. (ll. 133–6)

This was the particular passage of which the exact wording was not revealed in print until 1914. From the way the offending last couplet – in all the older printings of the poem and indeed for more than a century since Goethe wrote them – was editorially mutilated or simply expunged altogether, we may conclude that the provocative intention of this climactic stanza was widely recognized. The juxtaposition of the phallus and the central symbol of Christianity could hardly be viewed otherwise than as an openly defiant, polemical gesture by a 'decided non-Christian' ('dezidierter Nicht-Christ') as Goethe liked to call himself.

Goethe was painfully aware of the difficulty of naming the penis in German. Precisely this difficulty of finding an acceptable German word for that indispensible requisite of the mature and uninhibited poetry he sought to write had prompted him earlier to a notorious unpublished epigram in the best Priapean tradition, apparently written during his visit to Venice in 1790.[41] In *The Diary*, the word he chose for 'der Schwanz' was 'der Iste' – to rhyme with 'Christe'. It is the personified Latin demonstrative pronoun, meaning something like 'this thing here'. There has been some speculation about the origin and function of this curious lexical choice. But given the hieratic context, and in view of the central role assigned to the phallic god in the *Roman Elegies*, we may very well read the word *'Iste'* as metonymy – *pars pro toto* – for Priapus himself. A similarly blasphemous juxtaposition of the crucifix and Priapus, the god 'from Lampsacus' on the Hellespont (where his cult supposedly originated), occurs in another of the unpublished 'Venetian' epigrams: a display of bogus Christian relics on the eve of Good Friday provokes a hysterical girl to demand the production of one relic in particular, and the poet comments:

Armes Mädchen, was soll dir ein Teil des gekreuzigten Gottes?
Rufe den heilsamern Teil jenes von Lampsacus her.

Poor girl, what do you want with one of the crucified god's parts?
Call for the Lampsacan god's part, that will do you more good.[42]

In both texts the ancient idol has been raised as the heathen counterpart to the crucifix. We may recall here that Goethe's personal reaction to crucifixes and to the Christian cross in general appears to have been one of intense, if not indeed neurotic hatred, comparable to his equally visceral antagonism to Newton's theory of colours.

Whatever the secret implications of stanza XVII, the effects of this extraordinary flashback to the wild sexuality of youth are felt immediately. Mysteriously, the potency of the insomniac traveller is restored. The act of remembering is revealed to have the power to re-member in the physical sense as well. Yet the would-be lover does not wake his companion as we might have expected. Instead, in a surprising gesture of renunciation, he gets out of bed and resumes the other activity he was incapable of performing earlier: that of writing in his diary. The writer's powers, both sexual and creative, have been recovered. We should not simplify what the poem tells us of the reason for this new-found strength. It lies not merely in the fact that his thoughts turn again to his wife as such. Rather, it is the profoundly erotic recollection of his youthful passion for the woman who is now his wife. His bond with her evidently was and still is both erotic and personal, something much more complex and profound than the casual attraction to the pretty stranger. In Freudian terms we might say that the diarist's relationship to his wife is genital rather than phallic. It is this relationship that has acted as a 'magic knot' of the kind to which (l.116) he ruefully refers.

Once again the comparison with *Elective Affinities* is illuminating. The novel's central event occurs when Eduard and Charlotte, the husband and wife, have intercourse with each other – and not really with each other: he, in his imagination, is with his beloved Ottilie, and she with her would-be lover the Captain. But on this very occasion Eduard begets, and Charlotte conceives, a child – a son whose mysterious resemblance to his 'imagined' parents betrays the 'imagined' adultery committed by his biological parents in their hearts. In *The Diary*, on the other hand, the travelling husband's libido is strongly fixated on his absent wife and thus makes him at first unable to perform the intended seduction, and later disinclined to do so. His potency is restored, but the adultery does not happen. In the novel the absent beloved inwardly replaces the wife: in the poem the absent wife inwardly supplants her rival.

All this needs to be borne in mind if we are to understand adequately the ambiguities of the poem's concluding lines. By having the protagonist forego intercourse and resume his writing, Goethe has subverted the conventions of the *novella galante*. And now stanza XXIV, to the reader's even greater surprise, appears to offer a moral of deceptive simplicity: love, we are told, is a more powerful force for good than duty. But to read this pronouncement in the obvious, banal sense, as an edifying truism, would scarely do it justice as the conclusion of so daring and elaborate a text. The concluding lines lose their apparent simplicity as soon as we recognize that the two key words 'Pflicht' and 'Liebe' have a contextually more compelling significance here than would appear at first sight.

So far as 'Pflicht' is concerned, the context strongly suggests that in *The Diary* Goethe was using the word in its older, now extinct sense of specifically *marital* duty – as he does, for example, in *Elective Affinities*, *Torquato Tasso* and the ballad 'The God and the Dancing-

Girl'. (A comparable usage is the English cognate 'plight' in its older sense of 'promise', as in 'to plight one's troth'.) And looking beyond the context of Goethe's work we begin to realize that 'Pflicht' had been a key technical term in the legal and religious discourse on sexuality. We may safely assume that Goethe, himself a lawyer, would have been conscious of these implications. As Jean-Louis Flandrin has reminded us, duty in the sense of 'debt' (*debitum*) has been a central notion in theological teaching on marriage and sex ever since St Paul and St Jerome.[43] Essentially, the concept of duty served to regulate marital sex. Recognizing the existence of desire, the medieval Church fathers placed husband and wife under the obligation – the 'duty' – to satisfy each other's physical needs. At the same time, lust (*voluptas*) as an end in itself was forbidden and penalized, since, as St Jerome argued, 'nothing is so vile as to love one's wife as if she were a mistress'.[44]

Read in the light of this tradition, which around 1800 was still the dominant one, *The Diary* takes on a different, subtly subversive meaning. If 'Pflicht' is specifically the formal marital bond, the 'duty' to be not only faithful to one's wife but potent with her and indeed to procreate, and if 'Liebe' is not merely the conventional conjugal affection but specifically the elemental sexual desire, the libido – then Goethe's lines cannot be read as an endorsement of the centuries-old Christian teaching which, in fact, proscribed such desire. Nor can the poem be construed as an emphatic encomium of marital love or as a condemnation of extramarital love. Rather, it challenges us to a more profound reflection on the nature and the workings of desire. It distinguishes two sources of strength on which, when we 'stumble' in life (l. 190), we can rely: one is our commitment to the formal bond of marriage, but the other – love grounded in Eros – is a force more effective and reliable. Nature, under certain conditions, will prevail over culture, and triumph over it, as *Elective Affinities* demonstrates. *The Diary*, by rejecting the dominant hierarchy of values which exalts 'duty' over 'love', makes the same general point from a different perspective. As the *Roman Elegies* had done, *The Diary* affirms the very thing that Christianity has sought to contain and to regulate: the elemental, natural force of Eros.

Yet at the same time, and ironically, *The Diary* seems to suggest that while Eros is the driving-force of extra-marital love, it can also provide the most reliable basis for marriage. We can be prevented from 'stumbling' into infidelity not so much by a rational sense of moral obligation as by the mysterious psychosomatic workings of Eros itself. Again we may recall the parallel but contrasting situation in *Elective Affinities*: Eduard commits adultery on the level of fantasy, while on the literal level performing his conjugal duty; the diarist is about to commit adultery literally, but discovers that he could not do so without, in his fantasy, activating the erotic energy fuelled by his marriage. In neither case does an act of adultery actually occur, but in both cases the implied affirmation of marriage is couched in ambiguity and irony – a tragic irony in the novel, a conciliatory irony in the poem. There is ample justification, then, for characterizing *The Diary* as 'moral in tendency'. Eckermann was no doubt prompted to this remark by Goethe himself, who in the notes for his own *Annals* for the year 1810 had already described his new poem, in a striking phrase that resists translation, as 'erotisch-moralisch'.[45] Goethe well knew that his 'erotic morality' was ahead of his time. It foreshadows a similar posture in his great twentieth-century admirer Thomas Mann, who once commented on *Death in Venice* that its 'moral standpoint is of course one that can only be adopted ironically' ('freilich nur *ironice* ein-zunehmen').[46]

But notwithstanding the very modern ambiguities of Goethe's text, the conception of love celebrated in *The Diary* underscores once more the close kinship of this poem to the *Roman Elegies*. There, the force of Eros was celebrated in the figure of Priapus; here, the same force is represented by the 'Iste' of stanza XVII. What this seems to suggest is a strong underlying continuity of purpose. And we may conclude that the poem of 1810 can be traced back to the same project, the same motive that had inspired the *Elegies*: the intention to recover for Priapus his rightful place among the deities of the day and to reclaim his central place in poetry.

In historical perspective, *The Diary* may be seen as documenting a fundamental and lasting reorientation in the conception of ideal marriage. Though apparently concerned with the problem of adultery, Goethe's poem actually suggests a redefinition of marriage in which Eros is viewed as a moral force and as a more powerful and reliable foundation than the dictates and restrictions of 'duty'. Compared with *Elective Affinities*, which focuses on the moral dilemma of a declining social order, namely that of the landed gentry, *The Diary* opens up a more forward-looking perspective. It invokes specifically modern, bourgeois notions which in Germany had first been proposed by the young Romantics, notably by Friedrich Schlegel in his notoriously libertinistic novel *Lucinde* (1799). So far as England is concerned, a similar development was observed by Lawrence Stone in his magisterial study, *The Family, Sex and Marriage in England, 1500–1800*. According to Stone, a 'new ideal' of sexual ethics was gaining ascendancy towards the end of the eighteenth century – an ideal which Stone defines as 'fusion of marriage and sexual passion'. At its innermost core, Goethe's poem argues for precisely such a 'fusion of wife and mistress role'.[47]

Above all, however, *The Diary* stands out as a landmark in modern erotic poetry. It ventures, thematically speaking, into quite new territory: the psychology of sexual failure. It is interesting to note that in 1907 it was discussed by Freud and his colleagues at a meeting of the Vienna Psychoanalytical Society, when Maximilian Steiner read a paper 'On Functional Impotence'. Although not identified by title, the poem referred to by both Steiner and Freud is without a doubt *The Diary*; they may have read it in a scholarly reprint which had appeared in 1904.[48] Both cite 'the poem by Goethe' as illustration of a case of 'psychic impotence'. Freud differs from Steiner in his interpretation of the psychological causes of the sexual failure in *The Diary*. Sketching a typology of impotence, he identifies as the most interesting cases 'from a psychological point of view' those 'individuals whose sexual activity cannot dispense with the psychic component; whose phantasy life predominates; or, more generally, individuals whose sexual activity is of the feminine type. All of us civilized people' ('Kulturmenschen'), Freud observes, 'have some tendencies to psychic impotence'. On the basis of this general definition, Freud disagrees with Steiner who viewed the case as an example of how impotence can occur 'when one approaches a woman [. . .] with too deep respect'. Freud, by contrast, attributes the impotence to the fact that 'the libido is not available because it is bound to unconscious (repressed) ideas' or to another person, and specifically because of a 'fixation on the absent beloved'.[49] Freud, rather interestingly, refers here to the absent 'Geliebte' which means 'beloved' in a general sense, and 'mistress' in the specific sense. His remark thus goes some way towards confirming the reading of *The Diary* outlined above.

Among poets, Goethe seems to have been the first to treat the subject of impotence seriously and without prudishness. More important, *The Diary* participates fully in the decisive turn of European Romantic poetry to poetic self-consciousness. By reflecting on the interdependence of the love-act and the act of writing, it illuminates the condition of the modern poet in a post-priapean, no longer naive age. Furthermore, this poem succeeds where much so-called erotic writing disappoints: it is lighthearted but not affected, serious but not ponderous, and it is truly daring instead of being merely frivolous. Miraculously, Goethe kept his poem free of that philosophical and religious ballast with which the German Romantics – Friedrich Schlegel, for example, but also Novalis and Brentano – so burdened the literary treatment of sexuality. On the whole, Goethe also remained immune to the fascination of the power-games of sex, that obsession which drove his contemporary, the Marquis de Sade, to ever new explorations of the recesses of the human body and mind. However, like most erotic poetry written by men, Goethe's narrative contains more than a trace of phallocentric narcissism, though this is balanced and mitigated by the element of tenderness and delicacy in the narrator's treatment of the girl (ll. 111f., 167f.). *The Diary* is in fact a complex and profound human document of great sophistication – qualities which combine with the elegant virtuosity of its language to make it one of the most remarkable of all Goethe's poems.[50]

## NOTES

1. 'Further Advice for Young Poets', in Goethe's *Collected Works*, Vol. 3 (*Essays on Art and Literature*, edited by John Gearey, translated by E. and E. von Nardroff), Suhrkamp, New York, 1986, p. 209.

2. Conversation of 11 March 1828 with Eckermann, in *Conversations of Goethe with Eckermann and Soret*, translated by John Oxenford, 2 vols (Henry Bohn, London, 1850); an abridged edition of this translation is available in Everyman's Library (Dent, London, 1930 and North Point Press, San Francisco, 1984).

3. 'Further Advice for Young Poets', loc. cit., p. 209.

4. See *The Auto-biography of Goethe (Truth and Poetry: From My Own Life)*, translated by John Oxenford (Henry Bohn, London, 1848), pp. 445ff. For a modern edition of the same translation, with some amendments, see *The*

*Autobiography of Goethe*, introduction by George Sebba, 2 vols (Sidgwick & Jackson, London, 1971 and The University of Chicago Press, Chicago, 1974), vol. 2, pp. 134ff.

5. Avital Ronell, *Dictations. On Haunted Writing* (Indiana University Press, Bloomington, 1986), p. xv.

6. E. M. Wilkinson, article on Goethe in *The New Encyclopædia Britannica* (*Macropædia*). See also D. J. Enright, 'Goethe's "Roman Elegies"', *Scrutiny*, XV (1947/8), pp. 174–82; Theodore Ziolkowski, *The Classical German Elegy, 1795–1950* (Princeton University Press, Princeton, 1980), pp. 55–88; E. M. Wilkinson, 'Sexual Attitudes in Goethe's Life and Works', in *Goethe Revisited. A Collection of Essays*, edited by E. M. Wilkinson (John Calder, London, 1984), pp. 171–84.

7. See Hans Robert Jauss, *Towards an Aesthetic of Reception*, translated by Timothy Bahti, introduction by Paul de Man (University of Minnesota Press, Minneapolis, 1982), pp. 22ff.

8. See Karl Hehn, 'Quinque lineae amoris', *Germanisch-Romanische Monatsschrift*, XXIX (1941), pp. 236–47.

9. See Heinz Schlaffer, *Musa iocosa. Gattungspoetik und Gattungs-geschichte der erotischen Dichtung in Deutschland* [The Theory and History of Erotic Poetry in Germany] (Metzler, Stuttgart, 1971), pp. 159f.

10. Schlaffer's failure to account for this major erotic text by Goethe calls to mind an older, much less sophisticated study, Paul Kluckhohn's *Die Auffassung der Liebe in der Literatur des 18.Jahrhunderts und in der deutschen Romantik* [The Conception of Love in the Literature of the 18th Century and in German Romanticism] (Niemeyer, Halle, 1923), which managed somehow to avoid even the *Roman Elegies*.

11. Conversation with Eckermann, 25 February 1824.

12. See Dominik Jost, *Deutsche Klassik: Goethes 'Römische Elegien'* (Verlag Dokumentation, Pullach, 1974), p. 34.

13. On this point and on questions of Goethe's sexual life in general see Kurt R. Eissler, *Goethe. A Psychoanalytic Study, 1775–1786* (Wayne State University Press, Detroit, 1963), p. 1058. This work is also available in German translation (Roter Stern Verlag, Frankfurt, 1986).

14. *Faust*, lines 455–9, 1804f. Cf. *Faust (Part One)*, translated by David Luke (Oxford University Press, Oxford, 1987).

15. Conversation with Eckermann, 8 April 1829.

16. See *Goethes Briefwechsel mit seiner Frau* [Goethe's Correspondence with his wife], 2 vols, edited by Hans Gerhard Gräf (Rütten und Loening, Frankfurt, 1916). A judicious modern account of Goethe's relationship with Christiane can be found in Richard Friedenthal, *Goethe: His Life and Times* (Weidenfeld and Nicolson, London and The World Publishing Co., Cleveland

and New York, 1965) pp. 254–61. Cf. also Ernst Beutler, 'Christiane', in his *Essays um Goethe* (Dieterich'sche Verlagsbuchhandlung, fourth edition, Wiesbaden, 1948), pp. 251–64.

17. Letter to Karl Ludwig von Knebel, 1 January 1791.

18. Letter to Charlotte Schiller, 14–20 September 1794.

19. Letter to Friedrich Christian II, Duke of Schleswig-Holstein-Augustenburg, 5 July 1795.

20. For *Über naive und sentimentalische Dichtung* in English see (1) *German Aesthetics and Literary Criticism* (Winckelmann, Lessing, Hamann, Herder, Schiller, Goethe), edited and introduced by H. B. Nisbet (Cambridge University Press, Cambridge, 1985) or (2) *Naive and Sentimental Poetry* and *On the Sublime*, translated by Julius A. Elias (Frederick Ungar Publishing Co., New York, 1966). The relevant passage appears on p. 209 of (1) and pp. 143–4 of (2).

21. Letter to Christian Gottfried Körner, 20 July 1795.

22. The identity of the author or authors is uncertain, but cf. Vinzenz Buchheit, *Studien zum Corpus Priapeorum* (Beck, Munich, 1962), pp. 19ff., who argues persuasively for the cyclical organization of the poems and for a single authorship. For a convenient bilingual (Latin and German) edition see *Carmina Priapea. Gedichte an den Gartengott* [Poems to the Garden God], edited by B. Kytzler, translated by C. Fischer (Artemis, Zürich/Munich, 1978). An English translation (*Priapeia; or the Sportive Epigrams of divers Poets on Priapus*) was published under the pseudonym 'Neaniskos' (privately printed, 1890).

23. *Priapeia, sive diversorum poetarum in Priapum lusus* (1664), with commentaries by Caspar Schoppe and Joseph Scaliger. Goethe had his own copy, bound in one volume with Petronius's *Satyricon*.

24. It is also possible, however, that the dedicatee was Prince August (1747–1806), a younger brother of Duke Ernst II of Saxe-Gotha-Altenburg. August of Gotha was an enlightened and cultivated bachelor, interested in Latin poetry, who knew Herder, Goethe and other members of the Weimar circle.

25. Eissler, op. cit. (note 13 above), pp. 1340f.

26. The English translation of Goethe's essay by Moses Hadas (here quoted with slight alterations) is given in full by Eissler, ibid., pp. 1332–7.

27. It may be significant that Sir William Hamilton, a wealthy connoisseur who was British Ambassador to Naples at the time of Goethe's Italian journey, was interested in the cult of Priapus and had written an essay on its residual influence in modern Italian Catholicism (*Account of the Remains of the Worship of Priapus*, published privately in Italy, 1786). We know from the *Italian Journey* that when staying in Naples in 1787 Goethe was on friendly

Introduction

visiting terms with Hamilton and his young mistress Emma Hart (later Lady Hamilton), and was shown his collection of artistic curiosities. It is thus possible that the contact with Hamilton was a contributory stimulus to Goethe's Priapic studies.

28. See Michel Foucault, *A History of Sexuality*, vol. I: Introduction, translated by Robert Hurley (Pantheon, New York, 1978 and Allen Lane The Penguin Press, London, 1979).

29. See Harry Haile, 'Goethe. Erotica Romana', *Boston University Journal*, XXVII (1979), pp. 3–19. As far as I can see, Haile is the only previous translator of the *Roman Elegies* to present the complete 24-part cycle in the appropriate order, i.e. with the two Priapean poems as frame; ibid.

30. Buchheit, op. cit. (note 22 above), pp. 40ff.

31. See the useful survey of the poem's publication-history given by Siegfried Unseld, *'Das Tagebuch' Goethes und Rilkes 'Sieben Gedichte'* (Insel, Frankfurt, 1978), pp. 70ff. [Insel-Bücherei Nr. 1000].

32. See Albrecht Schöne, *Götterzeichen, Liebeszauber, Satanskult* [Omens, Love-magic and Satanism] (C. H. Beck, Munich, 1981).

33. For a more complete discussion of the philological evidence see Hans R. Vaget, *Goethe. Der Mann von 60 Jahren. Mit einem Anhang über Thomas Mann* [Goethe. The Man of 60. With an Appendix on Thomas Mann] (Athenäum, Königstein, 1982), pp. 29ff.

34. *Goethes Werke, herausgegeben im Auftrage der Großherzogin Sophie von Sachsen* [Goethe's Works, published by authority of the Grand Duchess Sophia of Saxony]; usually referred to as *WA* (*Weimarer Ausgabe* [Weimar Edition]). This was the first, and is still the most complete and authoritative, historical-critical edition of Goethe's entire literary output, scientific writings, diaries and letters; its 143 volumes and part-volumes were published from 1887 to 1919.

35. *WA*, vol. 5, ii, p. 345.

36. *WA*, vol. 53, p. 562.

37. Cf. *The Complete Poems of John Wilmot, Earl of Rochester*, edited by David M. Vieth (Yale University Press, New Haven and London, 1968), pp. 37–40.

38. Conversation with Eckermann, 25 February 1824.

39. Goethe, *Italian Journey* (1786–1788), translated by W. H. Auden and Elizabeth Mayer (Penguin Books, Harmondsworth, 1970, p. 361 and North Point Press, San Francisco, 1982, p. 358).

40. Cf. T. J. Reed's thoughtful observations in his *Goethe* (Oxford University Press, Oxford [Past Masters], 1984), p. 86f.

41. The 'Venetian Epigrams' (*Epigramme. Venedig 1790*), the fruit of Goethe's second and rather less inspiring Italian journey, contained a number

which he withheld from publication. The philological *jeu d'esprit* here in question reads:

Gib mir statt 'der Schwanz' ein ander Wort, o Priapus!
 Denn ich Deutscher, ich bin übel als Dichter geplagt,
Griechisch nennt ich dich φαλλός, das klänge doch prächtig den Ohren,
 Und lateinisch ist auch *mentula* leidlich ein Wort.
*Mentula* käme von *mens*, der Schwanz ist etwas von hinten,
 Und nach hinten war mir niemals ein froher Genuß.

Give me, Priapus, another name for it! 'Schwanz' is the German
 Word, devil take it, for 'tail'; what's a poor poet to do?
φαλλός I'd call it in Greek, that would be very fine and high-sounding;
 And a Roman would say *mentula*; that too would serve;
It's from *mens*, I suppose, meaning 'mind'. But a *tail*'s on one's backside:
 And backsidewise – well, that never was my kind of fun.

(*WA*, vol. 53, p. 15f.). Goethe's derivation of *mentula* from *mens* is interesting but fanciful.

42. *WA*, vol. 53, p.8.

43. See Jean-Louis Flandrin, *Le Sexe et l'Occident. Evolution des attitudes et des comportements* (Seuil, Paris, 1981).

44. See Jean-Louis Flandrin, 'Sex in married life in the early Middle Ages: the Church's teaching and behavioural reality', in *Western Sexuality. Practice and Precept in Past and Present Times*, edited by Philippe Ariès and André Béjin, translated by Anthony Forster (Blackwell, Oxford, 1985), p. 122.

45. *WA*, vol. 36, p. 399.

46. Cf. letter to C. M. Weber, 4 July 1920, in Thomas Mann, *Briefe 1889–1936*, edited and introduced by Erika Mann (S. Fischer Verlag, Frankfurt, 1962, pp. 176ff.; see also *Letters of Thomas Mann, 1889–1955*, selected and translated by Richard and Clara Winston, Secker and Warburg, London, 1970 and Alfred A. Knopf, New York, pp. 102ff.). Not surprisingly in view of the prominence of problematic sexual themes in his work, Mann was particularly interested in *The Diary*, which he seems to have first read in 1920. Echoes of it are clearly traceable in his later novels, including *The Magic Mountain*, *Joseph and his Brothers*, and *Dr Faustus*. The poem also plays a significant part in Mann's historical-fictional study of the elderly Goethe, *Lotte in Weimar*, in which (repeating Goethe's own phrase) he alludes to its 'erotic morality'. For further discussion of these connections see Vaget, op. cit. (note 33 above), pp. 140–73.

47. Cf. Lawrence Stone, *The Family, Sex and Marriage in England, 1500–1800* (Harper and Row, New York/London, 1977), pp. 527ff., 543ff.

48. *Das Tagebuch (1810). Vier unterdrückte römische Elegien. Nicolai auf Werthers Grab. Wortgetreue Nachdrucke, mit einer literarhistorischen Einleitung unter Benutzung eines bisher unbekannten Briefwechsels* [The Diary (1810). Four suppressed Roman Elegies. Nicolai on Werther's grave. Verbatim reprints, with a historical introduction based on a hitherto unknown correspondence], edited by Max Mendheim (Weigel, Leipzig, 1904). Mendheim, however, did not yet have access to the full text of stanza XVII.

49. *Minutes of the Vienna Psychoanalytic Society*, edited by Herman Nunberg and Ernst Federn, translated by M. Nunberg (International Universities Press, New York, 1962), vol. I: 1906–8, pp. 212–17.

50. It is a pleasure to acknowledge the many helpful suggestions I have received from friends and colleagues who were kind enough to read earlier versions of this essay: David Ball, Peter Bloom, Stanley Corngold, Andrew Ford, David Luke, Ann Philbrick, Judith Ryan.

# RÖMISCHE ELEGIEN

# ROMAN ELEGIES

# I

Hier ist mein Garten bestellt, hier wart ich die Blumen der Liebe,
  Wie sie die Muse gewählt, weislich in Beete verteilt.
Früchte bringenden Zweig, die goldenen Früchte des Lebens,
  Glücklich pflanz ich sie an, warte mit Freuden sie nun.
Stehe du hier an der Seite, Priap! ich habe von Dieben
  Nichts zu befürchten, und frei pflück und genieße wer mag.
Nur bemerke die Heuchler, entnervte, verschämte Verbrecher;
  Nahet sich einer und blinzt über den zierlichen Raum,
Ekelt an Früchten der reinen Natur, so straf ihn von hinten
10  Mit dem Pfahle, der dir rot von den Hüften entspringt.

# I*

Here my garden is growing, the flowers of Eros* I tend here;
　　They are the Muse's own choice, bedded out wisely they bloom.
Branches that bear ripe fruit, the golden fruit of the life-tree:
　　Gladly I planted them once, gladly I nurture them now.
Stand here beside them, Priapus! I've nothing to fear from
　　　　　　　　　　　　　　　　　　marauders;
　　Anyone's welcome, it's all free to be picked and enjoyed.
But keep the hypocrites out, those miscreants flaccid and shamefaced!
　　If one should dare to approach, peep at our charming domain,
Turn up his nose at the fruits of pure Nature, just punish his backside
　　With one thrust of that red stake-shaft that sprouts from your hips.　　10

* See pp. 125–33 for explanatory notes.

Saget, Steine, mir an, o sprecht, ihr hohen Paläste!
  Straßen, redet ein Wort! Genius, regst du dich nicht?
Ja, es ist alles beseelt in deinen heiligen Mauern,
  Ewige Roma; nur mir schweiget noch alles so still.
O wer flüstert mir zu, an welchem Fenster erblick ich
  Einst das holde Geschöpf, das mich versengend erquickt?
Ahn ich die Wege noch nicht, durch die ich immer und immer,
  Zu ihr und von ihr zu gehn, opfre die köstliche Zeit?
Noch betracht ich Kirch und Palast, Ruinen und Säulen,
20  Wie ein bedächtiger Mann schicklich die Reise benutzt.
Doch bald ist es vorbei; dann wird ein einziger Tempel,
  Amors Tempel, nur sein, der den Geweihten empfängt.
  Eine Welt zwar bist du, o Rom; doch ohne die Liebe
  Wäre die Welt nicht die Welt, wäre denn Rom auch nicht Rom.

## II

Speak to me, stones, oh say, you lofty palaces, tell me –
    Streets, are you lost for a word? Genius, how idly you sleep!*
Yes – though within your sacred walls, oh perennial city,
    All is alive and astir, still all is silent for me.
Who shall whisper the secret, and where one day at a window
    Shall I first see her, when first burn with love's life-giving fire?
Oh, those well-trodden paths that will lead me to her and from her,
    Squandering my hours away – can I not guess at them yet?
Still I am gazing at churches and palaces, ruins and columns,
    Carefully seeing the sights, as a good traveller should.        20
But all this will be over soon, and the city a temple –
    Love's great temple, and I'll be its initiate then.
Rome, though you are a whole world, yet a world without love would
                            be no world,
    And if there were no love, Rome would not even be Rome.

III

Mehr als ich ahndete schön, das Glück, es ist mir geworden;
    Amor führte mich klug allen Palästen vorbei.
Ihm ist es lange bekannt, auch hab ich es selbst wohl erfahren,
    Was ein goldnes Gemach hinter Tapeten verbirgt.
Nennet blind ihn und Knaben und ungezogen, ich kenne,
30    Kluger Amor, dich wohl, nimmer bestechlicher Gott!
Uns verführten sie nicht, die majestätschen Fassaden,
    Nicht der galante Balkon, weder das ernste Kortil.
Eilig ging es vorbei, und niedre zierliche Pforte
    Nahm den Führer zugleich, nahm den Verlangenden auf.
Alles verschafft er mir da, hilft alles und alles erhalten,
    Streuet jeglichen Tag frischere Rosen mir auf.
Hab ich den Himmel nicht hier? – Was gibst du, schöne Borghese,
    Nipotina, was gibst deinen Geliebten du mehr?
Tafel, Gesellschaft und Kors' und Spiel und Oper und Bälle,
40    Amorn rauben sie nur oft die gelegenste Zeit.
Ekel bleibt mir Gezier und Putz, und hebet am Ende
    Sich ein brokatener Rock nicht wie ein wollener auf?
Oder will sie bequem den Freund im Busen verbergen,
    Wünscht er von alle dem Schmuck nicht schon behend sie befreit?
Müssen nicht jene Juwelen und Spitzen, Polster und Fischbein
    Alle zusammen herab, eh er die Liebliche fühlt?
Näher haben wir das! Schon fällt dein wollenes Kleidchen,
    So wie der Freund es gelöst, faltig zum Boden hinab.
Eilig trägt er das Kind, in leichter linnener Hülle,
50    Wie es der Amme geziemt, scherzend aufs Lager hinan.
Ohne das seidne Gehäng und ohne gestickte Matratzen,
    Stehet es, zweien bequem, frei in dem weiten Gemach.
Nehme dann Jupiter mehr von seiner Juno, es lasse
    Wohler sich, wenn er es kann, irgend ein Sterblicher sein.
Uns ergötzen die Freuden des echten nacketen Amors
    Und des geschaukelten Betts lieblicher knarrender Ton.

# III

More than I ever had hoped, what happiness I have been granted!
    Love led me wisely through Rome, passing its palaces by.
He has long known, and I myself have learnt it the hard way,
    What the fine tapestries hide in all those bedrooms of gold.
Call Eros* blind if you like, and a boy, and wanton: I know him
    And his sagacity well, this incorruptible god.          30
Those majestic façades could not tempt us aside, nor the solemn
    Courtyards, the balconies well suited to nights of romance.
On we pressed, till at last a door both humble and charming
    Willingly welcomed the guide, welcomed the suppliant in.
Here there is nothing I lack, for he is a constant provider;
    Fresh are the roses that Love scatters each day on my path.
Is this not heaven itself? What more, fair Princess Borghese,*
    Fair Nipotina,* can you give for your lovers' delight?
Dinners and parties, walks or drives down the Corso, or card-games,
    Operas, dances – they waste so much good love-making time!    40
I have grown sick of adornments and finery: are not, when all's done,
    Skirts of brocade and of wool equally easy to lift?
How can a woman embrace her lover in comfort unless she
    First, at his eager behest, sheds all her dainty array?
Will he not want those jewels and laces, that whalebone and quilted
    Satin discarded at once, freeing her for his caress?
We make short work of all that! – In a trice I unfasten this simple
    Woollen dress, and it drops, slips in its folds to the floor.
Quickly, cajolingly, like a good nurse, I carry my darling –
    Only a light linen shift covers her now – to the bed.    50
Here are no curtains of silk, no embroidered mattresses; freely
    In the wide bedroom it stands, ample in width to take two.
Now not Jupiter's pleasure in Juno's embraces is greater,
    And no mortal's content vies, I will wager, with mine!
Ours is the true, the authentic, the naked Love; and beneath us,
    Rocking in rhythm, the bed creaks the dear song of our joy.

Ehret, wen ihr auch wollt! Nun bin ich endlich geborgen!
    Schöne Damen und ihr, Herren der feineren Welt,
Fraget nach Oheim und Vetter und alten Muhmen und Tanten,
60    Und dem gebundnen Gespräch folge das traurige Spiel.
Auch ihr übrigen fahret mir wohl, in großen und kleinen
    Zirkeln, die ihr mich oft nah der Verzweiflung gebracht.
Wiederholet, politisch und zwecklos, jegliche Meinung,
    Die den Wandrer mit Wut über Europa verfolgt.
So verfolgte das Liedchen *Malbrough* den reisenden Briten
    Einst von Paris nach Livorn, dann von Livorno nach Rom,
Weiter nach Napel hinunter; und wär er nach Smyrna gesegelt,
    Malbrough! empfing ihn auch dort! Malbrough! im Hafen
                                  das Lied.
Und so mußt ich bis jetzt auf allen Tritten und Schritten
70    Schelten hören das Volk, schelten der Könige Rat.
Nun entdeckt ihr mich nicht so bald in meinem Asyle,
    Das mir Amor der Fürst, königlich schützend, verlieh.
Hier bedecket er mich mit seinem Fittich; die Liebste
    Fürchtet, römisch gesinnt, wütende Gallier nicht;
Sie erkundigt sich nie nach neurer Märe, sie spähet
    Sorglich den Wünschen des Manns, dem sie sich eignete, nach.
Sie ergetzt sich an ihm, dem freien, rüstigen Fremden,
    Der von Bergen und Schnee, hölzernen Häusern erzählt;
Teilt die Flammen, die sie in seinem Busen entzündet,
80    Freut sich, daß er das Gold nicht wie der Römer bedenkt.
Besser ist ihr Tisch nun bestellt; es fehlet an Kleidern,
    Fehlet am Wagen ihr nicht, der nach der Oper sie bringt.
Mutter und Tochter erfreun sich ihres nordischen Gastes,
    Und der Barbare beherrscht römischen Busen und Leib.

# IV

*Now at last I am home and dry! Take your flattery elsewhere,
  My fair ladies, my fine gentlemen of the *beau monde*!
Chatter politely about your old aunts and uncles and cousins,
  Then let some tedious game follow the elegant talk.                    60
Goodbye all of you, social circles and gatherings, great and
  Small! How often you've half driven me out of my mind!
Travellers barely escape your political vain repetitions,
  Right across Europe one runs from their relentless pursuit.
Thus the English were plagued by the song *Malbrouk** on their
                                                          travels:
  Paris and Leghorn and Rome rang with it: southwards they fled,
Only to hear it in Naples; and even in far-distant Smyrna
  They would have sailed into port to a great cry of 'Malbrouk'!
So, hitherto, wherever I went, I would hear all the gossip,
  Hear them all cursing the mob, cursing the folly of kings.*           70
But you'll not easily find out now the retreat I have fled to;
  For Prince Eros, my host, royally shelters me here.
Under his wings I am hidden, along with my darling; she fears no
  Gallic frenzy,* I know she's a true Roman at heart.
She has no ears for the latest political rumours; she only
  Cares for the man of her choice, watching his wishes and needs.
She is delighted by him, this free and vigorous stranger,
  And with his tales about snow, mountains, and houses of wood;
She has kindled a fire in his heart, and shares it, rejoicing
  Too in his liberal purse (men are so mean here in Rome).              80
Now she eats better than ever before, and has plenty of dresses;
  Drives to the opera now, fetched in an elegant coach.
Mother and daughter are pleased with their northern guest, and a
                                                          Roman
  Bosom and body lie now under barbarian rule.

43

# V

Laß dich, Geliebte, nicht reun, daß du mir so schnell dich ergeben!
  Glaub es, ich denke nicht frech, denke nicht niedrig von dir.
Vielfach wirken die Pfeile des Amor: einige ritzen,
  Und vom schleichenden Gift kranket auf Jahre das Herz.
Aber mächtig befiedert, mit frisch geschliffener Schärfe
90  Dringen die andern ins Mark, zünden behende das Blut.
In der heroischen Zeit, da Götter und Göttinnen liebten,
  Folgte Begierde dem Blick, folgte Genuß der Begier.
Glaubst du, es habe sich lange die Göttin der Liebe besonnen,
  Als im Idäischen Hain einst ihr Anchises gefiel?
Hätte Luna gesäumt, den schönen Schläfer zu küssen,
  O, so hätt ihn geschwind, neidend, Aurora geweckt.
Hero erblickte Leandern am lauten Fest, und behende
  Stürzte der Liebende sich heiß in die nächtliche Flut.
Rhea Silvia wandelt, die fürstliche Jungfrau, der Tiber
100  Wasser zu schöpfen, hinab, und sie ergreifet der Gott.
So erzeugte die Söhne sich Mars! – Die Zwillinge tränket
  Eine Wölfin, und Rom nennt sich die Fürstin der Welt.

Darling, do not regret the promptness of your surrender!
  I think no less of you now, you have not lost my respect.
Eros has arrows that work many ways: some merely will scratch us,
  And as the slow venom acts, so the heart sickens for years.
But there are others, strong-feathered and freshly pointed and
                                    sharpened –
  Right to the marrow they pierce, quickly they kindle the blood.       90
In the heroic age, when a god fell in love with a goddess,
  Passion was born at a glance, and was assuaged in a trice.
Do you suppose that Venus herself, when she fancied Anchises*
  In the Idaean grove, pondered for long what to do?
Did the Moon-goddess think twice when she kissed the fair sleeping
                                    Endymion?*
  No! for the envious Dawn soon would have waked him instead.
At the loud festival Hero set eyes on Leander:* and that same
  Night he plunged into the sea, hot with impatient desire.
Rhea Sylvia,* the royal virgin, went down to the Tiber
  Fetching water, and Mars snatched her up into his arms;              100
Thus the War-god fathered his sons. Twin brothers a she-wolf
  Suckled, the founders of Rome: Rome now is queen of the world.

Fromm sind wir Liebende, still verehren wir alle Dämonen,
Wünschen uns jeglichen Gott, jegliche Göttin geneigt.
Und so gleichen wir euch, o römische Sieger! Den Göttern
Aller Völker der Welt bietet ihr Wohnungen an,
Habe sie schwarz und streng aus altem Basalt der Ägypter,
Oder ein Grieche sie weiß, reizend, aus Marmor geformt.
Doch verdrießet es nicht die Ewigen, wenn wir besonders
110 Weihrauch köstlicher Art Einer der Göttlichen streun.
Ja, wir bekennen euch gern: es bleiben unsre Gebete,
Unser täglicher Dienst Einer besonders geweiht.
Schalkhaft, munter und ernst begehen wir heimliche Feste,
Und das Schweigen geziemt allen Geweihten genau.
Eh an die Ferse lockten wir selbst durch gräßliche Taten
Uns die Erinnyen her, wagten es eher, des Zeus
Hartes Gericht am rollenden Rad und am Felsen zu dulden,
Als dem reizenden Dienst unser Gemüt zu entziehn.
Diese Göttin, sie heißt *Gelegenheit*; lernet sie kennen!
120 Sie erscheinet euch oft, immer in andrer Gestalt.
Tochter des Proteus möchte sie sein, mit Thetis gezeuget,
Deren verwandelte List manchen Heroen betrog.
So betriegt nun die Tochter den Unerfahrnen, den Blöden:
Schlummernde necket sie stets, Wachende fliegt sie vorbei;
Gern ergibt sie sich nur dem raschen, tätigen Manne,
Dieser findet sie zahm, spielend und zärtlich und hold.
Einst erschien sie auch mir, ein bräunliches Mädchen, die Haare
Fielen ihr dunkel und reich über die Stirne herab,
Kurze Locken ringelten sich ums zierliche Hälschen,
130 Ungeflochtenes Haar krauste vom Scheitel sich auf.
Und ich verkannte sie nicht, ergriff die Eilende, lieblich
Gab sie Umarmung und Kuß bald mir gelehrig zurück.
O wie war ich beglückt! – Doch stille, die Zeit ist vorüber,
Und umwunden bin ich, römische Flechten, von euch.

Lovers are pious: we worship all supernatural beings,
    Gods and goddesses all, humbly their favour we beg.
Thus we resemble the conquering Romans, for they too would offer
    Homes to the whole world's gods, gods of all peoples alike,
Whether Egyptians have carved them austerely from blackest old basalt
    Or they'd been fashioned by Greeks, marble and gleaming and
                                   white.
But the Immortals will not be incensed if as lovers we scatter
    Choicest of incense to one goddess we chiefly revere.          110
For we must gladly confess there is one whom we supplicate daily –
    Homage to one above all others we ardently pay.
Roguish and merry and grave are the rites of our secret observance,
    And a strict silence we keep, as all initiates must.
Rather by horrible deeds we ourselves would call up the Furies
    Hot on our heels, or risk Jupiter's sentence of doom
And endure to be whirled on a wheel or chained to a cliff-face,*
    Than be unmindful of this service that holds us in thrall.
Our dear goddess is called *Opportunity*: do you not know her?
    Often she comes to you, each time in a different guise.          120
She is the daughter of Proteus,* perhaps, engendered with Thetis,*
    Whose self-altering skill baffled the heroes of old.
Thus now their daughter deceives the inexperienced, the dullard,
    Flirting with any who nap, fleeting past all who keep watch.
Only to active resolute spirits she gladly surrenders:
    With such a man she is tame, playful and tender and kind.
Thus it was that one day she appeared to me,* as a dark-haired
    Girl: an abundance of locks tumbled down over her brow,
Shorter ringlets entwined her delicate neck, and unbraided
    Hair rose boldly in waves over the crown of her head.          130
And I knew her, I seized her as she went hurrying by me;
    Apt in response, she returned kiss and embrace with a will.
Oh, how happy I was!   But enough, that time is no longer,
    And I am captive and bound now, Roman tresses, by you.

# VII

Froh empfind ich mich nun auf klassischem Boden begeistert;
Vor- und Mitwelt spricht lauter und reizender mir.
Hier befolg ich den Rat, durchblättre die Werke der Alten
Mit geschäftiger Hand, täglich mit neuem Genuß.
Aber die Nächte hindurch hält Amor mich anders beschäftigt;
140 Werd ich auch halb nur gelehrt, bin ich doch doppelt beglückt.
Und belehr ich mich nicht, indem ich des lieblichen Busens
Formen spähe, die Hand leite die Hüften hinab?
Dann versteh ich den Marmor erst recht; ich denk und vergleiche,
Sehe mit fühlendem Aug, fühle mit sehender Hand.
Raubt die Liebste denn gleich mir einige Stunden des Tages,
Gibt sie Stunden der Nacht mir zur Entschädigung hin.
Wird doch nicht immer geküßt, es wird vernünftig gesprochen;
Überfällt sie der Schlaf, lieg ich und denke mir viel.
Oftmals hab ich auch schon in ihren Armen gedichtet
150 Und des Hexameters Maß leise mit fingernder Hand
Ihr auf den Rücken gezählt. Sie atmet in lieblichem Schlummer,
Und es durchglühet ihr Hauch mir bis ins Tiefste die Brust.
Amor schüret die Lamp indes und denket der Zeiten,
Da er den nämlichen Dienst seinen Triumvirn getan.

Now on classical soil I stand, inspired and elated:
    Past and present speak plain, charm me as never before.
Here I follow the counsels and busily thumb through the writings
    Of the ancients,* and each day with increasing delight.
But at the love-god's behest, by night my business is different;
    Half of my scholarship's lost, yet I have double the fun.      140
And is not this education, to study the shape of her lovely
    Breasts, and down over her hip slide my adventuring hand?
Marble comes doubly alive for me then, as I ponder, comparing,
    Seeing with vision that feels, feeling with fingers that see.
What if my darling deprive me of some few hours of daytime?
    Hours of night as a rich recompense she can bestow.
Though we spend some of them kissing, we spend others sensibly
                         talking,
    And when she sinks into sleep, wakeful and thoughtful I lie.
Often I even compose my poetry in her embraces,
    Counting hexameter beats, tapping them out on her back      150
Softly, with one hand's fingers. She sweetly breathes in her slumber,
    Warmly the glow of her breath pierces the depths of my heart.
Eros recalls, as he tends our lamp, how he did the same service
    For his Triumvirs,* the three poets of Love, long ago.

'Kannst du, o Grausamer! mich in solchen Worten betrüben?
    Reden so bitter und hart liebende Männer bei euch?
Wenn das Volk mich verklagt, ich muß es dulden! und bin ich
    Etwa nicht schuldig? Doch ach! schuldig nur bin ich mit dir!
Diese Kleider, sie sind der neidischen Nachbarin Zeugen,
160    Daß die Witwe nicht mehr einsam den Gatten beweint.
Bist du ohne Bedacht nicht oft bei Mondschein gekommen,
    Grau, im dunkeln Surtout, hinten gerundet das Haar?
Hast du dir scherzend nicht selbst die geistliche Maske gewählet?
    Solls ein Prälate denn sein! gut, der Prälate bist du.
In dem geistlichen Rom, kaum scheint es zu glauben, doch schwör ich:
    Nie hat ein Geistlicher sich meiner Umarmung gefreut.
Arm war ich leider! und jung, und wohlbekannt den Verführern;
    Falconieri hat mir oft in die Augen gegafft,
Und ein Kuppler Albanis mich, mit gewichtigen Zetteln,
170    Bald nach Ostia, bald nach den vier Brunnen gelockt.
Aber wer nicht kam, war das Mädchen. So hab ich von Herzen
    Rotstrumpf immer gehaßt und Violettstrumpf dazu.
Denn ''ihr Mädchen bleibt am Ende doch die Betrognen'',
    Sagte der Vater, wenn auch leichter die Mutter es nahm.
Und so bin ich denn auch am Ende betrogen! Du zürnest
    Nur zum Scheine mit mir, weil du zu fliehen gedenkst.
Geh! Ihr seid der Frauen nicht wert! Wir tragen die Kinder
    Unter dem Herzen, und so tragen die Treue wir auch;

'How can you hurt me by saying such things? Are lovers so cruel?
  Do all you men from the north talk in this hard, bitter way?
Public blame I must bear without complaining, for that I'm
  Guilty how can I deny? – but it is only with you!
These fine clothes are proof to my envious neighbour, she knows now
  That I'm no longer alone, mourning the husband I lost.*          160
Have you not often enough come here, unthinking, by moonlight,
  Grey, in a long dark coat, hair done in clerical style,
Not in a pigtail? You chose the disguise, you practical joker!
  So it's a prelate I love? Yes – you're my prelate, who else?
In this priest-ridden city – believe it or not, but I'll swear it –
  Who has had favours from me? Never a priest in all Rome!
Yes, I was poor, and young, and well known to seducers; and often
  Falconieri* would cast eyes on me, often some pimp
Of Albani's* would try to entice me to Quattro Fontane
  Or to Ostia – they'd bring messages heavy with coin;          170
But did I go? Not I! For in fact those clerical gaiters
  Always gave me the creeps, scarlet and purple* alike.
For as my father would say (though my mother would look on the
                                         bright side):
  "It's you girls, after all, who are the dupes in the end!"
And so it proves; in the end you too have deceived me. Your anger's
  Only a pretext, a sham; you want to leave me, I know.
Go, then! You men are not worthy of women; we carry your children
  Under our hearts, and it's there, there we bear faith to you too.

Aber ihr Männer, ihr schüttet mit eurer Kraft und Begierde
Auch die Liebe zugleich in den Umarmungen aus!'
Also sprach die Geliebte und nahm den Kleinen vom Stuhle,
    Drückt' ihn küssend ans Herz, Tränen entquollen dem Blick.
Und wie saß ich beschämt, daß Reden feindlicher Menschen
    Dieses liebliche Bild mir zu beflecken vermocht!
Dunkel brennt das Feuer nur augenblicklich und dampfet,
    Wenn das Wasser die Glut stürzend und jählings verhüllt;
Aber sie reinigt sich schnell, verjagt die trübenden Dämpfe,
    Neuer und mächtiger dringt leuchtende Flamme hinauf.

But you menfolk, when you embrace us you spill all your strength out,
    All your desire out at once – and your love goes the same way.'      180
Thus my darling reproached me, with tears in her eyes, and she lifted
    Her little boy* from his chair, kissing him, hugging him tight.
There I sat, so ashamed to have let such malice and slander
    Poison my mind with mistrust, spoiling an image so dear.
Fire burns smoky and dark when a sudden deluge of water
    Dashes its ardour, but soon blazes up brightly again;
In a mere moment it clears, driving off the vapours that dulled it –
    Then with what vigour, what fresh brilliance its flames are revived!

O wie fühl ich in Rom mich so froh! gedenk ich der Zeiten,
190    Da mich ein graulicher Tag hinten im Norden umfing,
Trübe der Himmel und schwer auf meine Scheitel sich senkte,
    Farb- und gestaltlos die Welt um den Ermatteten lag,
Und ich über mein Ich, des unbefriedigten Geistes
    Düstre Wege zu spähn, still in Betrachtung versank.
Nun umleuchtet der Glanz des helleren Äthers die Stirne;
    Phöbus rufet, der Gott, Formen und Farben hervor.
Sternhell glänzet die Nacht, sie klingt von weichen Gesängen,
    Und mir leuchtet der Mond heller als nordischer Tag.
Welche Seligkeit ward mir Sterblichem! Träum ich? Empfänget
200    Dein ambrosisches Haus, Jupiter Vater, den Gast?
Ach! hier lieg ich und strecke nach deinen Knieen die Hände
    Flehend aus. O vernimm, Jupiter Xenius, mich!
Wie ich hereingekommen, ich kanns nicht sagen: es faßte
    Hebe den Wandrer und zog mich in die Hallen heran.
Hast du ihr einen Heroen herauf zu führen geboten?
    Irrte die Schöne? Vergib! Laß mir des Irrtums Gewinn!
Deine Tochter Fortuna, sie auch! Die herrlichsten Gaben
    Teilt als ein Mädchen sie aus, wie es die Laune gebeut.
Bist du der wirtliche Gott? O dann so verstoße den Gastfreund
210    Nicht von deinem Olymp wieder zur Erde hinab!
'Dichter! wohin versteigest du dich?' – Vergib mir; der hohe
    Kapitolinische Berg ist dir ein zweiter Olymp.
Dulde mich, Jupiter, hier, und Hermes führe mich später,
    Cestius' Mal vorbei, leise zum Orkus hinab.

Oh, how happy I feel here in Rome, when I think of the old days –
   Dull grey days, till I fled from the imprisoning north!       190
Leaden lugubrious skies weighed down on me, bowing my spirits:
   Colour and shape there was none in that whole wearisome world.*
There, wrapped up in myself, I explored in silent moroseness
   Gloomy and shadowy paths of my unsatisfied mind.
Now in this shining ether a brighter radiance surrounds me:
   Here, at the sun-god's behest, colours and forms have appeared.
Here the nights are brilliant with stars and full of soft music,
   And the moonlight outglows lustreless northerly day.
Can a mere mortal enjoy such bliss? Am I dreaming? Oh father
   Jupiter, am I a guest in your ambrosial halls?       200
Ah, I lie and extend my hands as a suppliant to you,
   Here at your knees: oh hear, hear me, guest-honouring Jove!*
Heaven knows how I got in – the goddess of Youth* must have
                             snatched me
   Up, as I wandered on earth, into your palace on high.
Did you command her to bring some hero, and did the fair Hebe
   Make some mistake? Then let me profit from that, by your grace!
See, your daughter Fortuna, she too is a generous-hearted
   Girl, and how sweet are the gifts lavished on men by her whims!
Are you the god of Hospitality?* Do not reject me
   Then, oh Olympian host, hurling me back down to earth!       210
'Poet! what flights of fancy are these?' – Forgive me; your home from
   Home, the Capitoline Hill, high as Olympus it stands.
Jupiter, let me stay here! until Hermes* quietly leads me
   Down past Cestius' tomb,* down to the land of the dead.

# X

Wenn du mir sagst, du habest als Kind, Geliebte, den Menschen
    Nicht gefallen, und dich habe die Mutter verschmäht,
Bis du größer geworden und still dich entwickelt, ich glaub es:
    Gerne denk ich mir dich als ein besonderes Kind.
Fehlet Bildung und Farbe doch auch der Blüte des Weinstocks,
    Wenn die Beere, gereift, Menschen und Götter entzückt.

220

# X

When you were little, my darling, you tell me nobody liked you –
  Even your mother, you say, scorned you, until as the years
Passed, you quietly grew and matured; and I can believe it –
  It's rather pleasant to think you were a strange little child.
For though the flower of a vine may be still unformed and lack lustre,
  In the ripe grape it yields nectar for gods and for men.          220

XI

Herbstlich leuchtet die Flamme vom ländlich geselligen Herde,
  Knistert und glänzet, wie rasch! sausend vom Reisig empor.
Diesen Abend erfreut sie mich mehr; denn eh noch zur Kohle
  Sich das Bündel verzehrt, unter die Asche sich neigt,
Kommt mein liebliches Mädchen. Dann flammen Reisig und Scheite,
  Und die erwärmete Nacht wird uns ein glänzendes Fest.
Morgen frühe geschäftig verläßt sie das Lager der Liebe,
  Weckt aus der Asche behend Flammen aufs neue hervor.
Denn vor andern verlieh der Schmeichlerin Amor die Gabe,
230  Freude zu wecken, die kaum still wie zu Asche versank.

# XI

Now on the rustic hearth an autumnal welcoming fire glows,
  Kindled from crackling wood, brilliant with uprushing flame.
And tonight it delights me still more, for this bundle of twigs will
  Still be burning, not yet crumbled to ember and ash,
When my darling arrives. Then twigs and faggots will blaze up,
  And we shall make the night warm – what a fine feast it will be!
Early tomorrow she'll busily rise from the bed of our loving;
  Quickly the ashes she'll stir, soon the bright flame she'll renew.
For this especial gift Love gave to my dearest of charmers:
  Pleasure no sooner burns low than she can wake it again.          230

Alexander und Cäsar und Heinrich und Friedrich, die Großen,
    Gäben die Hälfte mir gern ihres erworbenen Ruhms,
Könnt ich auf Eine Nacht dies Lager jedem vergönnen;
    Aber die armen, sie hält strenge des Orkus Gewalt.
Freue dich also, Lebendger, der lieberwärmeten Stätte,
    Ehe den fliehenden Fuß schauerlich Lethe dir netzt.

## XII

Alexander and Caesar and Henry and Frederick,* those great kings,
 Gladly would yield up to me, each of them, half of his fame,
If by my leave he might lie in this bed even one little night long;
 But, poor souls, they are dead; Hades imprisons them all.
Therefore rejoice, living man, in the place that is warm with your
                                                       loving:
 Cold on your shuddering foot Lethe's dread water will lap.

Euch, o Grazien, legt die wenigen Blätter ein Dichter
    Auf den reinen Altar, Knospen der Rose dazu,
Und er tut es getrost. Der Künstler freuet sich seiner
240    Werkstatt, wenn sie um ihn immer ein Pantheon scheint.
Jupiter senket die göttliche Stirn, und Juno erhebt sie;
    Phöbus schreitet hervor, schüttelt das lockige Haupt;
Trocken schauet Minerva herab, und Hermes, der leichte,
    Wendet zur Seite den Blick, schalkisch und zärtlich zugleich.
Aber nach Bacchus, dem weichen, dem träumenden, hebet Cythere
    Blicke der süßen Begier, selbst in dem Marmor noch feucht.
Seiner Umarmung gedenket sie gern und scheinet zu fragen:
    Sollte der herrliche Sohn uns an der Seite nicht stehn?

# XIII*

These few leaves are a poet's oblation, oh Graces: on your pure
   Altar he lays them, and these rosebuds he offers as well,
And he has done this boldly. An artist is proud of his workshop
   When he looks round it and sees such an assembly of gods.      240
Jupiter bows his majestic head, and Juno holds hers high;
   Phoebus Apollo strides forth, shaking the locks from his brow;
And Minerva looks sternly down – and here's light-footed Hermes
   Casting a sidelong glance, roguish, yet tender as well.
But on soft Bacchus, the dreamer, the gaze of the lovely Cythere
   Falls with sweet longing; her eyes even in marble are moist.
She remembers his ardent embrace, and seems to be asking:
   'Where is our glorious son? Here at our side he should stand!'

Hörest du, Liebchen, das muntre Geschrei den Flaminischen Weg her?
250    Schnitter sind es; sie ziehn wieder nach Hause zurück,
Weit hinweg. Sie haben des Römers Ernte vollendet,
    Der für Ceres den Kranz selber zu flechten verschmäht.
Keine Feste sind mehr der großen Göttin gewidmet,
    Die, statt Eicheln, zur Kost goldenen Weizen verlieh.
Laß uns beide das Fest im stillen freudig begehen!
    Sind zwei Liebende doch sich ein versammeltes Volk.
Hast du wohl je gehört von jener mystischen Feier,
    Die von Eleusis hieher frühe dem Sieger gefolgt?
Griechen stifteten sie, und immer riefen nur Griechen,
260    Selbst in den Mauern Roms: 'Kommt zur geheiligten Nacht!'
Fern entwich der Profane; da bebte der wartende Neuling,
    Den ein weißes Gewand, Zeichen der Reinheit, umgab.
Wunderlich irrte darauf der Eingeführte durch Kreise
    Seltner Gestalten; im Traum schien er zu wallen: denn hier
Wanden sich Schlangen am Boden umher, verschlossene Kästchen,
    Reich mit Ähren umkränzt, trugen hier Mädchen vorbei,
Vielbedeutend gebärdeten sich die Priester und summten;
    Ungeduldig und bang harrte der Lehrling auf Licht.
Erst nach mancherlei Proben und Prüfungen ward ihm enthüllet,
270    Was der geheiligte Kreis seltsam in Bildern verbarg.
Und was war das Geheimnis! als daß Demeter, die große,
    Sich gefällig einmal auch einem Helden bequemt,

Do you hear, darling, the merry shouts from the Via Flaminia?*
  Those are the homeward bound reapers – their journey was long,    250
Coming to gather the Roman harvest, coming to crown great
  Ceres* with garlands, a task which our own citizens scorn.
For that goddess is honoured with feasts no longer, whose bounty
  Bettered our acorn fare, gave us the gold of her wheat.
So let us gladly, you and I, do her homage in private:
  Surely two partners in love are a whole nation in joy!
Have you perhaps heard tell of those ancient mystical rites which
  Followed the Conqueror's path, back from Eleusis* to Rome?
They had been founded by Greeks, and even here in this city
  Those were still Greeks who cried: 'This is the holy night, come!'    260
Then the profane would depart, and the waiting novice would
                                     tremble,
  Clad, as befitting the pure, in his white candidate's robe.
Strangely the newcomer wandered then, encircled by figures
  Strange to behold – he walked as in a dream-world: for here
Serpents writhed on the ground around him, and young girls passed
                                      him –
  Close-locked caskets they bore, richly with corn-ears wreathed;
Priests mysteriously moved and chanted in rites full of meaning;
  Here the learner in awe eagerly waited for light.
Not until after much testing and many ordeals did they teach him
  What in that circle, in signs wondrous and sacred, lay hid.    270
And what was the great secret? No more than that mighty Demeter,
  She too, once, had obliged, bowed to a hero's desire –

Als sie Jasion einst, dem rüstigen König der Kreter,
Ihres unsterblichen Leibs holdes Verborgne gegönnt.
Da war Kreta beglückt! das Hochzeitbette der Göttin
Schwoll von Ähren, und reich drückte den Acker die Saat.
Aber die übrige Welt verschmachtete; denn es versäumte
Über der Liebe Genuß Ceres den schönen Beruf.
Voll Erstaunen vernahm der Eingeweihte das Märchen,
280    Winkte der Liebsten – Verstehst du nun, Geliebte, den Wink?
Jene buschige Myrte beschattet ein heiliges Plätzchen!
Unsre Zufriedenheit bringt keine Gefährde der Welt.

When long ago to the stalwart Jasion,* king of the Cretans,
　　She disclosed her divine limbs and their hidden delights.
Fortunate Crete! for that island, the wedding-couch of the goddess,
　　Teemed with corn from then on, heavy its fields were with wheat,
But all the rest of the world had to languish, for Ceres neglected
　　In the enjoyment of love what she was wont to provide.
And the initiate, amazed on hearing this tale, made a signal
　　To his beloved – do you, darling, know now what it meant?　　　280
Look, there's a sacred spot which those myrtle-bushes are hiding:
　　We can be happy in there, and not endanger mankind.

Amor bleibet ein Schalk, und wer ihm vertraut, ist betrogen!
  Heuchelnd kam er zu mir: 'Diesmal nur traue mir noch.
Redlich mein ichs mit dir: du hast dein Leben und Dichten,
  Dankbar erkenn ich es wohl, meiner Verehrung geweiht.
Siehe, dir bin ich nun gar nach Rom gefolget; ich möchte
  Dir im fremden Gebiet gern was Gefälliges tun.
Jeder Reisende klagt, er finde schlechte Bewirtung;
290  Welchen Amor empfiehlt, köstlich bewirtet ist er.
Du betrachtest mit Staunen die Trümmern alter Gebäude
  Und durchwandelst mit Sinn diesen geheiligten Raum.
Du verehrest noch mehr die werten Reste des Bildens
  Einziger Künstler, die stets ich in der Werkstatt besucht.
Diese Gestalten, ich formte sie selbst! Verzeih mir, ich prahle
  Diesmal nicht; du gestehst, was ich dir sage, sei wahr.
Nun du mir lässiger dienst, wo sind die schönen Gestalten,
  Wo die Farben, der Glanz deiner Erfindungen hin?
Denkst du nun wieder zu bilden, o Freund? Die Schule der Griechen
300  Blieb noch offen, das Tor schlossen die Jahre nicht zu.
Ich, der Lehrer, bin ewig jung, und liebe die Jungen.
  Altklug lieb ich nicht! Munter! Begreife mich wohl!
War das Antike doch neu, da jene Glücklichen lebten!
  Lebe glücklich, und so lebe die Vorzeit in dir!
Stoff zum Liede, wo nimmst du ihn her? Ich muß dir ihn geben,
  Und den höheren Stil lehret die Liebe dich nur.'
Also sprach der Sophist. Wer widerspräch ihm? und leider
  Bin ich zu folgen gewöhnt, wenn der Gebieter befiehlt. –
Nun, verräterisch hält er sein Wort, gibt Stoff zu Gesängen,
310  Ach! und raubt mir die Zeit, Kraft und Besinnung zugleich;
Blick und Händedruck, und Küsse, gemütliche Worte,
  Silben köstlichen Sinns wechselt ein liebendes Paar.

Eros was ever a rogue, and his promises fool the unwary.
   Subtly dissembling he came: 'Trust me just this once!' he said,
'I mean well by you – you have devoted your life and your writings
   To my service and fame, and this I gratefully note.
Now, having followed you even to Rome, as you see, in this foreign
   Country I should, in some way, like to do you a good turn.
Travellers always complain they are not treated as a guest should be;
   But they get all they could wish when they are sponsored by Love.    290
Here you stare with amazement at ancient buildings in ruins,
   And in this sacred place thoughtful and curious you roam;
Even more you revere the noble fragments of certain
   Rare creators, whom I often would visit at work –
For it was I who shaped and created for them! Forgive me,
   This is no idle boast; you must acknowledge its truth.
Since you became more lax in my service, have not your inventions
   Lost all their colour and form, lustre and beauty? My friend,
Would you now practise your art once more? The school of the
                                    Greeks is
   Open as ever; the years pass, yet its doors never closed.    300
I, the teacher, can never grow old; I love all who are youthful –
   Lively of heart, young in mind! be so, and mark my words well:
When they lived and enjoyed, it was new, that world you call ancient:
   Now, by enjoying your life, make the past live on in you!
Where shall you find a theme for your songs? It is Love who
                                provides it,
   And in the loftier style there's no tuition like mine.'
Thus this sophist addressed me; and who should gainsay him? Alas, I
   Only too gladly obey when I receive his commands.
Well, he is true to his word, yet false! I have matter for poems;
   But where, alas, is my time, where are my senses and strength?    310
Now two lovers, with pressure of hands, with glances and kisses,
   Murmur in tender exchange syllables precious to hear.

Da wird Lispeln Geschwätz, wird Stottern liebliche Rede:
    Solch ein Hymnus verhallt ohne prosodisches Maß.
Dich, Aurora, wie kannt ich dich sonst als Freundin der Musen!
    Hat, Aurora, dich auch Amor, der lose, verführt?
Du erscheinest mir nun als seine Freundin, und weckest
    Mich an seinem Altar wieder zum festlichen Tag.
Find ich die Fülle der Locken an meinem Busen! Das Köpfchen
320    Ruhet und drücket den Arm, der sich dem Halse bequemt.
Welch ein freudig Erwachen, erhieltet ihr, ruhige Stunden,
    Mir das Denkmal der Lust, die in den Schlaf uns gewiegt! –
Sie bewegt sich im Schlummer und sinkt auf die Breite des Lagers,
    Weggewendet; und doch läßt sie mir Hand noch in Hand.
Herzliche Liebe verbindet uns stets und treues Verlangen,
    Und den Wechsel behielt nur die Begierde sich vor.
Einen Druck der Hand, ich sehe die himmlischen Augen
    Wieder offen. – O nein! laßt auf der Bildung mich ruhn!
Bleibt geschlossen! ihr macht mich verwirrt und trunken, ihr raubet
330    Mir den stillen Genuß reiner Betrachtung zu früh.
Diese Formen, wie groß! wie edel gewendet die Glieder!
    Schlief Ariadne so schön: Theseus, du konntest entfliehn?
Diesen Lippen ein einziger Kuß! O Theseus, nun scheide!
    Blick ihr ins Auge! Sie wacht! – Ewig nun hält sie dich fest.

Lisping and stammering turn into talk, into sweetest of converse –
  Rhapsodies, hymns of a kind, but not the kind you can scan.
Goddess of Dawn, hitherto I have known you as 'friend of the
                                         Muses'!*
  Have Love's blandishing wiles won the dawn-goddess as well?
Now you come to my window as *his* paramour, and I waken
  Here at his altar again, greeting the splendour of day.
Over my breast her locks fall full and abundant; her head droops
  Heavy, her neck fits snug on my encircling arm.                    320
Pleasure that rocked us to sleep, have the quiet hours preserved you?*
  Could a memorial be raised? Then with what joy I can wake!
In her slumber she moves and turns away from me, sinks down
  On the wide bed, but her hand still she leaves lying in mine.
Tenderest love is the bond between us, and faithfullest longing;
  Only our mutual desire varies, as appetites do.
If I so much as press on her hand, I shall see her enchanting
  Eyes reopen – ah no! let me still study her shape!
Eyes, stay closed! you make me confused and drunken, too soon you
  Bring to an end this pure, quiet, contemplative joy.               330
Look, how splendid these forms, how nobly moulded her limbs are!
  Did Ariadne* sleep so? Theseus, oh how could you leave?
Only one kiss on those lovely lips – flee, Theseus! she wakes! Now
  You are her captive – her gaze holds you for ever in thrall.

Zünde mir Licht an, Knabe! – 'Noch ist es hell. Ihr verzehret
  Öl und Docht nur umsonst. Schließet die Läden doch nicht!
Hinter die Häuser entwich, nicht hinter den Berg, uns die Sonne!
  Ein halb Stündchen noch währts bis zum Geläute der Nacht.' –
Unglückseliger! geh und gehorch! Mein Mädchen erwart ich.
340  Tröste mich, Lämpchen, indes, lieblicher Bote der Nacht!

## XVI

Light the lamp for me, boy! – 'But it's daylight still! you are wasting
   Oil and wick, sir, in vain. Why close the shutters just yet?
Look, the sun is not under the hill, only under the housetops!
   There'll be another half-hour yet till the angelus rings.'
Wretch! obey me at once! My beloved is coming! – And meanwhile,
   Till she is here, little lamp, comfort me, herald of night!     340

Zwei gefährliche Schlangen, vom Chore der Dichter gescholten,
    Grausend nennt sie die Welt Jahre die tausende schon,
Python, dich, und dich, Lernäischer Drache! Doch seid ihr
    Durch die rüstige Hand tätiger Götter gefällt.
Ihr zerstöret nicht mehr mit feurigem Atem und Geifer
    Herde, Wiesen und Wald, goldene Saaten nicht mehr.
Doch welch ein feindlicher Gott hat uns im Zorne die neue
    Ungeheure Geburt giftigen Schlammes gesandt?
Überall schleicht er sich ein, und in den lieblichsten Gärtchen
350    Lauert tückisch der Wurm, packt den Genießenden an.
Sei mir, hesperischer Drache, gegrüßt, du zeigtest dich mutig,
    Du verteidigtest kühn goldener Äpfel Besitz!
Aber dieser verteidiget nichts — und wo er sich findet,
    Sind die Gärten, die Frucht keiner Verteidigung wert.
Heimlich krümmet er sich im Busche, besudelt die Quellen,
    Geifert, wandelt in Gift Amors belebenden Tau.
O! wie glücklich warst du, Lucrez! du konntest der Liebe
    Ganz entsagen und dich jeglichem Körper vertraun.
Selig warst du, Properz! dir holte der Sklave die Dirnen
360    Vom Aventinus herab, aus dem Tarpeischen Hain.
Und wenn Cynthia dich aus jenen Umarmungen schreckte,
    Untreu fand sie dich zwar; aber sie fand dich gesund.
Jetzt wer hütet sich nicht, langweilige Treue zu brechen!
    Wen die Liebe nicht hält, hält die Besorglichkeit auf.
Und auch da, wer weiß! gewagt ist jegliche Freude,
    Nirgend legt man das Haupt ruhig dem Weib in den Schoß.
Sicher ist nicht das Ehbett mehr, nicht sicher der Ehbruch;
    Gatte, Gattin und Freund, eins ist im andern verletzt.
O! der goldenen Zeit! da Jupiter noch, vom Olympus,
370    Sich zu Semele bald, bald zu Kallisto begab.

You were two perilous serpents, reviled with one voice by the poets,
    And for long ages the world shuddered on hearing your names:
Python,* and you, Lernaean Hydra!* But luckily you're both
    Dead, struck down by the strong hands of adventuresome gods.
Now your fiery breath and your venomous spittle no longer
    Blast our forests and flocks, blight our rich acres of corn.
But, alas! what god in his fury and malice has sent us
    This new monster,* this plague born of the poisonous mire?
Nowhere is safe from its creeping intrusion, it lurks in the loveliest
    Gardens, this treacherous worm strikes in the act of our joy!     350
Hail, Hesperian dragon!* at least you bravely and fiercely
    Guarded those apples of gold, out in the uttermost west.
But this creature has nothing to guard, for gardens where he hides,
    And any fruit he has touched, they're not worth guarding at all.
Secretly there in the bushes he squirms, befouling the waters,
    Slavering poison and death into Love's life-giving dew.
Happy Lucretius!* you could renounce romantic attachment,
    And without cause for alarm clasp any body you chose.
Slaves brought you your consenting bedmates, lucky Propertius,*
    Down from the Aventine Hill, out of the Tarpeian Grove;     360
And if Cynthia caught you with one, then though you had wronged
                                            her
    By being faithless, at least nothing was wrong with your health.
Who does not hesitate now to break faith with a tedious mistress?
    Love may not hold us, but sheer caution will make us think twice.
Even at home, who knows! Not a single pleasure is risk-free;
    Who in his own wife's lap now lays a confident head?
Neither in wedlock now nor out of it can we be certain;
    Mutually noxious we are, husband and lover and wife.
Oh for that golden age, when Jove would descend from Olympus,
    Visiting Semele's* place, paying Callisto* a call!     370

Ihm lag selber daran, die Schwelle des heiligen Tempels
    Rein zu finden, den er liebend und mächtig betrat.
O! wie hätte Juno getobt, wenn im Streite der Liebe
    Gegen sie der Gemahl giftige Waffen gekehrt.
Doch wir sind nicht so ganz, wir alte Heiden, verlassen,
    Immer schwebet ein Gott über der Erde noch hin,
Eilig und geschäftig, ihr kennt ihn alle, verehrt ihn!
    Ihn den Boten des Zeus, Hermes, den heilenden Gott.
Fielen des Vaters Tempel zu Grund, bezeichnen die Säulen
    Paarweis kaum noch den Platz alter verehrender Pracht,
Wird des Sohnes Tempel doch stehn und ewige Zeiten
    Wechselt der Bittende stets dort mit dem Dankenden ab.
Eins nur fleh ich im stillen, an euch ihr Grazien wend ich
    Dieses heiße Gebet tief aus dem Busen herauf:
Schützet immer mein kleines, mein artiges Gärtchen, entfernet
    Jegliches Übel von mir; reichet mir Amor die Hand,
O! so gebet mir stets, sobald ich dem Schelmen vertraue,
    Ohne Sorgen und Furcht, ohne Gefahr den Genuß.

380

He himself, in that sacred temple, required a clean welcome
　　When he came to its door, entering in amorous might.
What a great fuss would Juno* have made, if she'd found that with
　　　　　　　　　　　　　　　　　poisoned
　　Weapons her husband fought, back in the conjugal bed! –
But we old heathen sinners are not completely abandoned;
　　We can still call on one god – he hovers over the earth,
Busy and swift: you all know his name, so pay him due homage!
　　He, Jove's messenger-boy, Mercury – he knows the cure.*
Though his father's great temples have fallen, with pairs of old
　　　　　　　　　　　　　　　　columns
　　Scarcely still marking the place of the majestic old cult,　　　380
Yet young Mercury's temple will stand, and his suppliants enter
　　Still, while others depart gratefully, world without end.
One petition to you, oh Graces, I offer in private!
　　Grant this one fervent request, made from the depths of my heart:
Always protect the neat little garden I cherish, and always
　　Fend off diseases from me; when I'm invited by Love
And when I trust myself to him, that rogue, may my pleasure be ever
　　Carefree, and never with fear, never with danger be mixed!

Cäsarn wär ich wohl nie zu fernen Britannen gefolget,
390    Florus hätte mich leicht in die Popine geschleppt!
Denn mir bleiben weit mehr die Nebel des traurigen Nordens,
    Als ein geschäftiges Volk südlicher Flöhe verhaßt.
Und noch schöner von heut an seid mir gegrüßet, ihr Schenken,
    Osterien, wie euch schicklich der Römer benennt;
Denn ihr zeigtet mir heute die Liebste, begleitet vom Oheim,
    Den die Gute so oft, mich zu besitzen, betriegt.
Hier stand unser Tisch, den Deutsche vertraulich umgaben;
    Drüben suchte das Kind neben der Mutter den Platz,
Rückte vielmals die Bank und wußt es artig zu machen,
400    Daß ich halb ihr Gesicht, völlig den Nacken gewann.
Lauter sprach sie, als hier die Römerin pfleget, kredenzte,
    Blickte gewendet nach mir, goß und verfehlte das Glas.
Wein floß über den Tisch, und sie, mit zierlichem Finger,
    Zog auf dem hölzernen Blatt Kreise der Feuchtigkeit hin.
Meinen Namen verschlang sie dem ihrigen; immer begierig
    Schaut ich dem Fingerchen nach, und sie bemerkte mich wohl.
Endlich zog sie behende das Zeichen der römischen Fünfe
    Und ein Strichlein davor. Schnell, und sobald ichs gesehn,
Schlang sie Kreise durch Kreise, die Lettern und Ziffern zu löschen;
410    Aber die köstliche *Vier* blieb mir ins Auge geprägt.
Stumm war ich sitzen geblieben, und biß die glühende Lippe,
    Halb aus Schalkheit und Lust, halb aus Begierde, mir wund.
Erst noch so lange bis Nacht! dann noch vier Stunden zu warten!
    Hohe Sonne, du weilst, und du beschauest dein Rom!
Größeres sahest du nichts und wirst nichts Größeres sehen,
    Wie es dein Priester Horaz in der Entzückung versprach.
Aber heute verweile mir nicht, und wende die Blicke
    Von dem Siebengebirg früher und williger ab!

# XVIII

Caesar would hardly have got me to travel to far-away Britain;
  Florus's taverns in Rome would have been more to my taste.\*          390
If one must choose between mists of the dismal north and a host of
  Hard-working southern fleas, give me the fleas any day!
And I have now even greater cause to salute and to praise you,
  *Osterie*\* – as inns here are so fittingly called:
For my darling today came to one of you, brought by her uncle,\*
  Whom so often she tricks when she finds ways to meet me.
Here was our table, with its familiar circle of Germans;
  And at a table near by, next to her mother, she sat.
Clever girl! she shifted the bench and so rearranged things
  That I could half see her face, and her whole neck was in view.       400
Raising her voice rather high for a Roman girl, she did the honours,
  Gave me a sidelong look, poured the wine, missing her glass.
Over the table it spilled,\* and with dainty finger she doodled –
  There, on the wet wooden page, circles of moisture she traced.
My name she mingled with hers; I eagerly followed her finger,
  Watching its every stroke, and she well knew that I did.
Quickly at last she inscribed a Roman 'five', with an upright
  'One' in front of it – then, when I had seen this, at once
With arabesque-like lines she effaced the letters and numbers,
  But left stamped on my mind's eye the delectable 'IV'.\*              410
I had sat speechless, biting my burning lip till it bled; half
  Mischievous pleasure I felt, half was aflame with desire.
Still so long until nightfall, and four more hours then of waiting!
  High sun, pausing to gaze down at your city of Rome,
Nothing you ever have seen has been greater, and nothing you
                                        will see;
  This was the truth that your priest, Horace, in rapture foretold.\*
Only today do not linger, consent to be brief in your survey,
  Sooner than usual to take leave of the fair Seven Hills!

79

Einem Dichter zuliebe verkürze die herrlichen Stunden,
420     Die mit begierigem Blick selig der Maler genießt;
Glühend blicke noch schnell zu diesen hohen Fassaden,
    Kuppeln und Säulen zuletzt und Obelisken herauf;
Stürze dich eilig ins Meer, um morgen früher zu sehen,
    Was Jahrhunderte schon göttliche Lust dir gewährt:
Diese feuchten, mit Rohr so lange bewachsnen Gestade,
    Diese mit Bäumen und Busch düster beschatteten Höhn.
Wenig Hütten zeigten sie erst; dann sahst du auf einmal
430     Sie vom wimmelnden Volk glücklicher Räuber belebt.
Alles schleppten sie drauf an diese Stätte zusammen;
    Kaum war das übrige Rund deiner Betrachtung noch wert.
Sahst eine Welt hier entstehn, sahst dann eine Welt hier in
                                        Trümmern,
    Aus den Trümmern aufs neu fast eine größere Welt!
Daß ich diese noch lange von dir beleuchtet erblicke,
    Spinne die Parze mir klug langsam den Faden herab.
Aber sie eile herbei, die schön bezeichnete Stunde! –
    Glücklich! hör ich sie schon? Nein; doch ich höre schon Drei.
So, ihr lieben Musen, betrogt ihr wieder die Länge
440     Dieser Weile, die mich von der Geliebten getrennt.
Lebet wohl! Nun eil ich, und fürcht euch nicht zu beleidgen;
    Denn ihr Stolzen, ihr gebt Amorn doch immer den Rang.

Show a poet this favour, and shorten the hours of splendid
  Brightness, which painters' eyes drink so insatiably in;                420
Flash but a farewell glance at these lofty façades, at these columns;
  Gleam on the obelisks, gleam now on the domes, and begone!
Swiftly plunge into the sea and rise early tomorrow to hasten
  Back to this ageless sight, feast for the gaze of a god.
See, these moist river-banks that so long were covered with rushes,
  And these dark wooded hills, shadowed with bushes and trees –
Only a few huts stood there at first, then a flourishing tribe of
  Fortunate robbers* arrived, peopling the place in a trice.
Here they gathered, and here their loot and wealth they assembled;
  This you observed – little else seemed to you worthy of note.        430
This was the birth of a world, and you saw it then perish in ruins,
  But from the ruins perhaps something still greater arose.
Oh, that I yet may for long behold this world in your radiance,
  Wisely and slow let the Fates spin out the thread of my life!
But that hour she so sweetly assigned, oh, let it come quickly!
  Does it already strike four? No; but with joy I hear three.
So, dear Muses, once more, as the tedious hours divided
  Me from my darling, how well you have beguiled them away!
Farewell now! I'll make haste to my tryst, and not fear to offend
                                                                you;
  You may be proud, but you grant precedence always to Love.          440

'Warum bist du, Geliebter, nicht heute zur Vigne gekommen?
  Einsam, wie ich versprach, wartet ich oben auf dich.' –
Beste, schon war ich hinein; da sah ich zum Glücke den Oheim
  Neben den Stöcken, bemüht, hin sich und her sich zu drehn.
Schleichend eilt ich hinaus! – 'O welch ein Irrtum ergriff dich!
  Eine Scheuche nur wars, was dich vertrieb! Die Gestalt
Flickten wir emsig zusammen aus alten Kleidern und Rohren;
  Emsig half ich daran, selbst mir zu schaden bemüht.' –
Nun, des Alten Wunsch ist erfüllt; den losesten Vogel
450  Scheucht' er heute, der ihm Gärtchen und Nichte bestiehlt.

'Darling, why didn't you come today to the vineyard to meet me?
  I waited there by myself, just as I promised I would!'
'Sweetheart, I came – but just then, by good luck, I caught sight of
                                        your uncle
  Busily watching the vines, turning his head to and fro;
So I crept out again quickly!' 'My dear, what a silly mistake! That's
  Only the scarecrow – so that scared you away! We all worked
Stitching the dummy together with sticks and old clothes, and I
                                        helped too
  Making it. So all that work brought me bad luck in the end!'
Well, the old man should be glad today to have startled a bird more
  Wanton than any, whose wiles steal both his fruit and his niece.    450

Manche Töne sind mir Verdruß, doch bleibet am meisten
  Hundegebell mir verhaßt; kläffend zerreißt es mein Ohr.
Einen Hund nur hör ich sehr oft mit frohem Behagen
  Bellend kläffen, den Hund, den sich der Nachbar erzog.
Denn er bellte mir einst mein Mädchen an, da sie sich heimlich
  Zu mir stahl, und verriet unser Geheimnis beinah.
Jetzo, hör ich ihn bellen, so denk ich mir immer: sie kommt wohl!
  Oder ich denke der Zeit, da die Erwartete kam.

## XX

Many noises enrage me, but none, I think, is more odious
  Than the barking, the ear-splintering yapping of dogs.
Only my neighbour's dog is now an exception: so often
  Hearing his bark and his yelp, I am contented and glad.
For he barked at my darling once, when secretly she was
  Stealing a visit to me, and nearly gave us away.
Now, if I hear him bark, I always think: she must be coming!
  Or I remember the time when, long-awaited, she came.

Eines ist mir verdrießlich vor allen Dingen, ein andres
460    Bleibt mir abscheulich, empört jegliche Faser in mir,
Nur der bloße Gedanke. Ich will es euch, Freunde, gestehen:
    Gar verdrießlich ist mir einsam das Lager zu Nacht.
Aber ganz abscheulich ists, auf dem Wege der Liebe
    Schlangen zu fürchten, und Gift unter den Rosen der Lust,
Wenn im schönsten Moment der hin sich gebenden Freude
    Deinem sinkenden Haupt lispelnde Sorge sich naht.
Darum macht Faustine mein Glück; sie teilet das Lager
    Gerne mit mir, und bewahrt Treue dem Treuen genau.
Reizendes Hindernis will die rasche Jugend; ich liebe,
470    Mich des versicherten Guts lange bequem zu erfreun.
Welche Seligkeit ists! wir wechseln sichere Küsse,
    Atem und Leben getrost saugen und flößen wir ein.
So erfreuen wir uns der langen Nächte, wir lauschen,
    Busen an Busen gedrängt, Stürmen und Regen und Guß.
Und so dämmert der Morgen heran; es bringen die Stunden
    Neue Blumen herbei, schmücken uns festlich den Tag.
Gönnet mir, o Quiriten! das Glück, und jedem gewähre
    Aller Güter der Welt erstes und letztes der Gott!

One thing I find more irksome than anything else, and another
  Thing I supremely abhor – it really curdles my blood,       460
Even the thought of it does. Let me tell you, my friends, what these
                                          two are:
  First, to sleep by myself irks me, I truly confess.
But what I utterly loathe is the fear that on pathways of pleasure,
  Under the roses of love, serpents and poison* may lurk.
This is the hideous thought which at moments of sweetest surrender,
  As I half swoon with delight, care whispers into my ear.
That is what makes me so happy to have Faustina: she gladly
  Sleeps with me, but she remains faithful, as I do to her.
Risks and checks may attract impetuous youth, but for my part
  Let me in comfort possess what is reliably mine.       470
What delight for us both! We kiss with confidence, safely
  Breathe the other's breath in, suck the dear life each from each.
Thus we enjoy the long nights together, we lie and we listen,
  Heart pressed to heart, as the wind storms and the rain gushes
                                        down,
Till dawn breaks, and the morning shines on us. Thus, as they pass,
                                        new
  Festive blossoms adorn every new hour of our day.
Oh, Rome's citizens, do not begrudge me such bliss! and to all men
  May Love grant it – this first, this crowning blessing of life.

Schwer erhalten wir uns den guten Namen, denn Fama
480    Steht mit Amorn, ich weiß, meinem Gebieter, in Streit.
Wißt auch ihr, woher es entsprang, daß beide sich hassen?
    Alte Geschichten sind das, und ich erzähle sie wohl.
Immer die mächtige Göttin, doch war sie für die Gesellschaft
    Unerträglich, denn gern führt sie das herrschende Wort;
Und so war sie von je, bei allen Göttergelagen,
    Mit der Stimme von Erz, Großen und Kleinen verhaßt.
So berühmte sie einst sich übermütig, sie habe
    Jovis herrlichen Sohn ganz sich zum Sklaven gemacht.
'Meinen Herkules führ ich dereinst, o Vater der Götter',
490    Rief triumphierend sie aus, 'wiedergeboren dir zu.
Herkules ist es nicht mehr, den dir Alkmene geboren;
    Seine Verehrung für mich macht ihn auf Erden zum Gott.
Schaut er nach dem Olymp, so glaubst du, er schaue nach deinen
    Mächtigen Knieen; vergib! nur in den Äther nach mir
Blickt der würdigste Mann; nur mich zu verdienen, durchschreitet
    Leicht sein mächtiger Fuß Bahnen, die keiner betrat;
Aber auch ich begegn ihm auf seinen Wegen, und preise
    Seinen Namen voraus, eh er die Tat noch beginnt.
Mich vermählst du ihm einst; der Amazonen Besieger
500    Werd auch meiner, und ihn nenn ich mit Freuden Gemahl!'
Alles schwieg; sie mochten nicht gern die Prahlerin reizen:
    Denn sie denkt sich, erzürnt, leicht was Gehässiges aus.
Amorn bemerkte sie nicht: er schlich beiseite; den Helden
    Bracht er mit weniger Kunst unter der Schönsten Gewalt.
Nun vermummt er sein Paar: ihr hängt er die Bürde des Löwen
    Über die Schultern und lehnt mühsam die Keule dazu,
Drauf bespickt er mit Blumen des Helden sträubende Haare,
    Reichet den Rocken der Faust, die sich dem Scherze bequemt.
So vollendet er bald die neckische Gruppe; dann läuft er,
510    Ruft durch den ganzen Olymp: 'Herrliche Taten geschehn!

Our good name is in danger, I fear; between Love who commands me
    And the goddess Repute* there is, I know, bitter strife.       480
And have you heard how it all began, that mutual hatred?
    It's an old story, you see, one that I might as well tell.
She is indeed a powerful goddess, but socially she was
    Quite impossible – too talkative, rasping away
With her clangorous voice – and each time the gods were assembled,
    All of them, great and small, heartily hated its sound.
Thus in her arrogance once she boasted as one of her conquests
    Jove's magnificent son: 'Hercules* now is my slave,*
Father Jupiter!' proudly she cried, 'and one day I'll bring him
    Up to Olympus with me, totally mine and reborn!      490
He is no longer Alcmene's* son, the hero you fathered;
    His devotion to me makes him a god upon earth.
When he looks up at us, not Jove's mighty knees are attracting
    His rapt gaze, as you think: no, excuse me! it is I
Whom this noblest of men looks heavenwards for, only I whom
    He would deserve as he strides paths never trodden before.
But I meet him as well on his ways, I go forward before him,
    Praising his name as he comes, heralding deeds still undone.
I shall demand him from you in marriage: the Amazon's victor*
    Shall be mine also – with joy I shall be Hercules' wife!'      500
All were silent, for none of them felt like provoking the loudmouth:
    When she is angered, her spite quickly breeds slanderous tales.
Only Eros evaded her notice by stealth; and with ease he
    Soon had her hero bewitched, to a fair lady* enthralled.
Then he transvested the pair, laboriously laying the lion's
    Pelt across Omphale's back, putting the club by her side.
Next, with flowers he decked the resisting hair of the hero –
    But with a distaff in hand, Hercules joined in the joke.
Thus the Love-god completed this teasing pose, and ran swiftly
    Through the Olympian halls, crying: 'Great deeds! Come and see!    510

Nie hat Erd und Himmel, die unermüdete Sonne
   Hat auf der ewigen Bahn keines der Wunder erblickt.'
Alles eilte; sie glaubten dem losen Knaben, denn ernstlich
   Hatt er gesprochen; und auch Fama, sie blieb nicht zurück.
Wer sich freute, den Mann so tief erniedrigt zu sehen,
   Denkt ihr! Juno. Es galt Amorn ein freundlich Gesicht.
Fama daneben, wie stand sie beschämt, verlegen, verzweifelnd!
   Anfangs lachte sie nur: 'Masken, ihr Götter, sind das!
Meinen Helden, ich kenn ihn zu gut! Es haben Tragöden
520   Uns zum besten!' Doch bald sah sie mit Schmerzen, er wars! –
Nicht den tausendsten Teil verdroß es Vulkanen, sein Weibchen
   Mit dem rüstigen Freund unter den Maschen zu sehn,
Als das verständige Netz im rechten Moment sie umfaßte,
   Rasch die Verschlungnen umschlang, fest die Genießenden hielt.
Wie sich die Jünglinge freuten! Merkur und Bacchus! sie beide
   Mußten gestehn: es sei, über dem Busen zu ruhn
Dieses herrlichen Weibes, ein schöner Gedanke. Sie baten:
   Löse, Vulkan, sie noch nicht! Laß sie noch einmal besehn.
Und der Alte war so Hahnrei, und hielt sie nur fester. –
530   Aber Fama, sie floh rasch und voll Grimmes davon.
Seit der Zeit ist zwischen den zweien der Fehde nicht Stillstand;
   Wie sie sich Helden erwählt, gleich ist der Knabe darnach.
Wer sie am höchsten verehrt, den weiß er am besten zu fassen,
   Und den Sittlichsten greift er am gefährlichsten an.
Will ihm einer entgehn, den bringt er vom Schlimmen ins
                              Schlimmste.
   Mädchen bietet er an; wer sie ihm töricht verschmäht,
Muß erst grimmige Pfeile von seinem Bogen erdulden;
   Mann erhitzt er auf Mann, treibt die Begierden aufs Tier.
Wer sich seiner schämt, der muß erst leiden; dem Heuchler
540   Streut er bittern Genuß unter Verbrechen und Not.

Never has heaven or earth or the tireless sun on its endless
   Course seen a wonder to beat this one that I'll show you now!'
And they all came, for the words of the mischievous knave had been
                                                   earnest,
   So they believed him; and she, Reputation, came with them as well.
Guess who was glad to behold her husband's bastard so humbled!
   Juno, of course; and on Love now she most graciously smiled.
But Reputation stood there ashamed, embarrassed, despairing.
   First she tried laughing it off: 'Gods, these are nothing but masks!
I know my hero only too well: we are being made fools of
   By mere actors!' But soon, stricken, she saw she was wrong! –          520
Vulcan* had felt not a thousandth part of her rage when he found his
   Wife with her martial friend, caught in the net on their bed,
By his cunning invention enmeshed at just the right moment,
   Clasped in it as they lay clutched, locked in their spasm of joy.
How that had pleased young Bacchus and Mercury! Both had
                                                   admitted
   What a fine thing it would be, if one could lie for a while
In the embrace of that lovely goddess. They had asked Vulcan:
   'Don't release her just yet! Let's have another good look!'
And the old man, having nothing to lose, kept his cuckolders
                                                   captive. –
   But Reputation now fled furiously from the scene;                      530
And ever since, she and Love have constantly warred with each other.
   Heroes whom she singles out, he at once marks for attack;
Those who are most devoted to her are the boy's surest victims,
   And the strict moralists, their peril is greater by far.
All who would flee from him fare the worst with this maker of
                                                   mischief:
   Girls he will offer them – if these they imprudently scorn,
Then indeed he will pierce their pride with his angriest arrows:
   Male he inflames for male, drives us to lust after beasts.
All who feel shame about Love he punishes: hypocrites have to
   Burn with bitter desires, driven to crime and despair.                 540

Aber auch sie, die Göttin, verfolgt ihn mit Augen und Ohren;
  Sieht sie ihn einmal bei dir, gleich ist sie feindlich gesinnt,
Schreckt dich mit ernstem Blick, verachtenden Mienen, und heftig
  Strenge verruft sie das Haus, das er gewöhnlich besucht.
Und so geht es auch mir: schon leid ich ein wenig; die Göttin,
  Eifersüchtig, sie forscht meinem Geheimnisse nach.
Doch es ist ein altes Gesetz: ich schweig und verehre;
  Denn der Könige Zwist büßten die Griechen, wie ich.

But Reputation pursues him too with sharpest of ears and
  Eyes: beware of her wrath if she once finds him with you!
Her stern looks and contempt will startle you – with a fierce rigour
  Fame will defame any house visited often by Love.
I too am learning this now, and the jealous goddess already
  Plagues me a little: she spies out my most secret delights.
So the old rule* holds good – I revere it in silence: for 'when their
  Mad kings quarrelled, the Greeks paid for it'; so too with me.

Zieret Stärke den Mann und freies mutiges Wesen,
550    Oh! so ziemet ihm fast tiefes Geheimnis noch mehr.
Städtebezwingerin du, Verschwiegenheit! Fürstin der Völker!
    Teure Göttin, die mich sicher durchs Leben geführt,
Welches Schicksal erfahr ich! Es löset scherzend die Muse,
    Amor löset, der Schalk, mir den verschlossenen Mund.
Ach, schon wird es so schwer, der Könige Schande verbergen!
    Weder die Krone bedeckt, weder ein phrygischer Bund
Midas' verlängertes Ohr; der nächste Diener entdeckt es,
    Und ihm ängstet und drückt gleich das Geheimnis die Brust.
In die Erde vergrüb er es gern, um sich zu erleichtern:
560    Doch die Erde verwahrt solche Geheimnisse nicht;
Rohre sprießen hervor und rauschen und lispeln im Winde:
    Midas! Midas, der Fürst, trägt ein verlängertes Ohr!
Schwerer wird es nun mir, ein schönes Geheimnis zu wahren;
    Ach, den Lippen entquillt Fülle des Herzens so leicht!
Keiner Freundin darf ichs vertraun: sie möchte mich schelten;
    Keinem Freunde: vielleicht brächte der Freund mir Gefahr.
Mein Entzücken dem Hain, dem schallenden Felsen zu sagen,
    Bin ich endlich nicht jung, bin ich nicht einsam genug.
Dir, Hexameter, dir, Pentameter, sei es vertrauet,
570    Wie sie des Tags mich erfreut, wie sie des Nachts mich beglückt.
Sie, von vielen Männern gesucht, vermeidet die Schlingen,
    Die ihr der Kühnere frech, heimlich der Listige legt;
Klug und zierlich schlüpft sie vorbei und kennet die Wege,
    Wo sie der Liebste gewiß lauschend begierig empfängt.
Zaudre, Luna, sie kommt! damit sie der Nachbar nicht sehe;
    Rausche, Lüftchen, im Laub! niemand vernehme den Tritt.
Und ihr, wachset und blüht, geliebte Lieder, und wieget
    Euch im leisesten Hauch lauer und liebender Luft,
Und entdeckt den Quiriten, wie jene Rohre geschwätzig,
580    Eines glücklichen Paars schönes Geheimnis zuletzt.

Strength, and a bold and liberal nature, are virtues a man needs;
   And even more, he must know how to keep things to himself.     550
Goddess Discretion! defeater of cities and ruler of peoples!
   Dear protectress, my sure guide through the perils of life,
See what a pass I am in! My lips are sealed, but the laughing
   Muse and the Love-god, that rogue, tempt me and loosen my tongue.
Ah, how hard it becomes to cover up royal disgraces!
   Midas* needs more than a crown, more than a Phrygian cap
If he would hide his ass-ears. His closest servant has seen them,
   And a secret so dire heavily weighs on his mind.
He'd like to bury it deep in the earth, for that would relieve him;
   But such secrets as this even the earth will not keep.     560
Reeds spring up, and when the wind blows they rustle and murmur:
   'Midas, Midas the king, Midas has long pointed ears!'
Now it is growing harder for me to keep a sweet secret;
   Ah, when the heart is so full, easily lips overflow!
Which of my friends can I tell? Not a woman, for she might reproach me;
   Not a man either, for he might be a rival to fear.
And to confide my joy to the grove, to the rocks and their echoes –
   That is for lonesome youth, that will not do at my age.
Listen, hexameter, listen, pentameter: you, then, shall hear it –
   How she delights me by day, how she enchants me by night!     570
Many men seek her favours and try to ensnare her, the bold ones
   Crudely, the cunning ones more subtly; but all she outwits.
Prudently, gracefully, she slips by, for she knows where her lover
   Ardently listens and waits, knows hidden ways to his arms.
Moonlight, oh hesitate now – she is coming: no neighbour must see her!
   Rustle the leaves, little breeze; no one must hear her approach!
And you, oh my beloved songs, may you blossom and flourish,
   Swaying in love's warm winds, rocked by their gentlest breath;
Chatter as those reeds did, and at last tell Rome all about us:
   Tell of two lovers whose glad secret is secret no more.     580

Hinten im Winkel des Gartens, da stand ich, der letzte der Götter,
    Rohgebildet, und schlimm hatte die Zeit mich verletzt.
Kürbisranken schmiegten sich auf am veralteten Stamme,
    Und schon krachte das Glied unter den Lasten der Frucht.
Dürres Gereisig neben mir an, dem Winter gewidmet,
    Den ich hasse, denn er schickt mir die Raben aufs Haupt,
Schändlich mich zu besudeln; der Sommer sendet die Knechte,
    Die, sich entladende, frech zeigen das rohe Gesäß.
Unflat oben und unten! ich mußte fürchten ein Unflat
590    Selber zu werden, ein Schwamm, faules verlorenes Holz.
Nun, durch deine Bemühung, o! redlicher Künstler, gewinn ich
    Unter Göttern den Platz, der mir und andern gebührt.
Wer hat Jupiters Thron, den schlechterworbnen, befestigt?
    Farb und Elfenbein, Marmor und Erz und Gedicht.
Gern erblicken mich nun verständige Männer, und denken
    Mag sich jeder so gern, wie es der Künstler gedacht.
Nicht das Mädchen entsetzt sich vor mir, und nicht die Matrone,
    Häßlich bin ich nicht mehr, bin ungeheuer nur stark.
Dafür soll dir denn auch halbfußlang die prächtige Rute
600    Strotzen vom Mittel herauf, wenn es die Liebste gebeut.
Soll das Glied nicht ermüden, als bis ihr die Dutzend Figuren
    Durchgenossen, wie sie künstlich Philänis erfand.

Once in the garden's far corner I stood, the last and the least god,
  Coarsely carved, and ill-used by the rude ravage of time.
Gourd-plant tendrils entwined my perishing trunk, and already
  My poor member had cracked under the weight of the fruit.
Broken branches lay by me, dry withered twigs for the winter;
  How I hate winter! that's when ravens, detestable birds,
Drop all their filth on my head; and in summer the insolent
                           gardeners
  Squat here relieving themselves, showing their ugly backsides.
Shit from upstairs and downstairs! I feared even I would be turning
  Into a spongy old turd, nothing but rotten waste wood.      590
Now, thanks to your good work, honest craftsman, I have been
                           granted
  My due place among gods, fitting for me and for all.
What has kept Jove on his ill-gotten throne, and established it
                           soundly?
  Colour and ivory, bronze, marble and poetry's art.
Now I'm a sight for intelligent men, they all like to imagine
  They themselves are as well made as the artist made me.
Girls are no longer shocked when they see me, and neither are
                           matrons,
  For I'm not hideous now, I'm just enormously strong.
Therefore I bless your magnificent central rod, may it always
  Stand up half a foot tall at your beloved's behest.      600
May your member not tire, until you have both done the dozen
  Figures Philaenis* describes, finished the dance of your joy.

# DAS TAGEBUCH

# THE DIARY

## DAS TAGEBUCH

*– aliam tenui, sed iam quum gaudia adirem,*
*Admonuit dominae deseruitque Venus.*

### I

Wir hören's oft und glauben's wohl am Ende:
Das Menschenherz sei ewig unergründlich,
Und wie man auch sich hin und wider wende,
So sei der Christe wie der Heide sündlich.
Das Beste bleibt, wir geben uns die Hände
Und nehmen's mit der Lehre nicht empfindlich;
Denn zeigt sich auch ein Dämon, uns versuchend,
So waltet was, gerettet ist die Tugend.

### II

Von meiner Trauten lange Zeit entfernet,
10  Wie's öfters geht, nach irdischem Gewinne,
Und was ich auch gewonnen und gelernet,
So hatt ich doch nur immer Sie im Sinne;
Und wie zu Nacht der Himmel erst sich sternet,
Erinnrung uns umleuchtet ferner Minne:
So ward im Federzug des Tags Ereignis
Mit süßen Worten Ihr ein freundlich Gleichnis.

# THE DIARY*

*– aliam tenui, sed iam quum gaudia adirem,
Admonuit dominae deseruitque Venus.\**

## I

The saying goes – it's true enough, no doubt –
That man's heart is for ever fathomless:
That Christians, though they turn and turn about,
Are sinners still, like pagans. Let's confess
As much, and all shake hands! We carry out
What Virtue bids us, only rather less;
Why fret? For when by some wild imp we're tempted
Another force prevails, and sin's preempted.

## II

It happened, as so often, travelling
For worldly profit, I'd been some time parted          10
From my true love; and many a useful thing
I'd done and learnt – but always, faithful-hearted,
Thinking of her. At night's first glittering
Of stars, remembered love's bright fire is started:
So too, I'd pen the doings of my day
In sweet words for my darling far away.

* See pp. 133–4 for explanatory notes.

## III

Ich eilte nun zurück. Zerbrochen sollte
Mein Wagen mich noch eine Nacht verspäten;
Schon dacht ich mich, wie ich zu Hause rollte,
20   Allein da war Geduld und Werk vonnöten.
Und wie ich auch mit Schmied und Wagner tollte,
Sie hämmerten, verschmähten viel zu reden.
Ein jedes Handwerk hat nun seine Schnurren.
Was blieb mir nun? Zu weilen und zu murren.

## IV

So stand ich nun! Der Stern des nächsten Schildes
Berief mich hin, die Wohnung schien erträglich.
Ein Mädchen kam, des seltensten Gebildes,
Das Licht erleuchtend. Mir ward gleich behäglich.
Hausflur und Treppe sah ich als ein Mildes,
30   Die Zimmerchen erfreuten mich unsäglich.
Den sündgen Menschen, der im Freien schwebet –
Die Schönheit spinnt, sie ist's die ihn umwebet.

## V

Nun setzt ich mich zu meiner Tasch und Briefen
Und meines Tagebuchs Genauigkeiten,
Um so wie sonst, wenn alle Menschen schliefen,
Mir und der Trauten Freude zu bereiten;
Doch weiß ich nicht, die Tintenworte liefen
Nicht so wie sonst in alle Kleinigkeiten:
Das Mädchen kam, des Abendessens Bürde
40   Verteilte sie gewandt mit Gruß und Würde.

## III

Now, hurrying back to her, misfortune struck
My homeward course: a broken wheel delayed me.
So soon I'd have been there! Now I was stuck.
O workmanship, what a droll trick you'd played me!  20
I cursed the smith, the wainwright and my luck;
They hammered on, and scant reply they made me.
I wait, they ply their mystery. What a crew!
But stay the night was all that I could do.


## IV

So there I stood. The nearest hostelry
Was called 'The Star'; it looked a decent place.
A girl appeared – a shapely rarity –
With lamp and light; my spirits rose apace.
The hallway and the stairs delighted me,
The little rooms seemed full of charm and grace.  30
When sinful mortals wander far from home,
Beauty's fine web may catch them as they roam.


## V

So I sat down to my portfolio,
My letters, and my diary's exact
Reports: nocturnal words, which I would show
As always to my dearest. Yet they lacked
Somehow tonight their usual easy flow;
The ink ran sluggish round each trifling fact.
The girl brought up my supper, greeted me
And laid it out with skill and dignity.  40

## VI

Sie geht und kommt; ich spreche, sie erwidert.
Mit jedem Wort erscheint sie mir geschmückter.
Und wie sie leicht mir nun das Huhn zergliedert,
Bewegend Hand und Arm, geschickt, geschickter –
Was auch das tolle Zeug in uns befiedert,
Genug, ich bin verworrner, bin verrückter,
Den Stuhl umwerfend spring ich auf und fasse
Das schöne Kind; sie lispelt: Lasse, lasse!

## VII

Die Muhme drunten lauscht, ein alter Drache,
50    Sie zählt bedächtig des Geschäfts Minute;
Sie denkt sich unten, was ich oben mache,
Bei jedem Zögern schwenkt sie frisch die Rute.
Doch schließe deine Türe nicht und wache,
So kommt die Mitternacht uns wohl zu Gute.
Rasch meinem Arm entwindet sie die Glieder,
Und eilet fort und kommt nur dienend wieder;

## VIII

Doch blickend auch! so daß aus jedem Blicke
Sich himmlisches Versprechen mir entfaltet.
Den stillen Seufzer drängt sie nicht zurücke,
60    Der ihren Busen herrlicher gestaltet.
Ich sehe, daß am Ohr, um Hals und Gnicke
Der flüchtgen Röte Liebesblüte waltet,
Und da sie nichts zu leisten weiter findet,
Geht sie und zögert, sieht sich um, verschwindet.

## VI

She comes and goes, and as we talk I'm stricken
With growing admiration for her charm.
I watch how cleverly she carves my chicken
With quick, deft movements of her hand and arm:
How my mad feathers sprout, my pulses quicken!
In short, my head's confused, my heart is warm,
And up I jump, knock the chair over, seize
The pretty creature – but she whispers: 'Please,

## VII

Not now! My aunt's downstairs, she listens when
I serve up here, and checks how long I stay;      50
She brandishes her rod, the old harridan,
And punishes each minute of delay.
But stay awake, don't lock your door, and then
When midnight comes, maybe we'll find a way.'
She wriggles free from my embrace, and slips
Back to her work; soon in again she trips

## VIII

To serve me – but her looks, how much they tell!
A heavenly promise blossoms from her eyes;
I watch her rounded bosom's splendid swell
As it is filled with little half-checked sighs;     60
And to her ears and throat and neck as well
I see the fleeting rosy love-flush rise.
She pauses then, finds all her duties done,
Hesitates, looks about her and is gone.

## IX

Der Mitternacht gehören Haus und Straßen,
Mir ist ein weites Lager aufgebreitet,
Wovon den kleinsten Teil mir anzumaßen
Die Liebe rät, die alles wohl bereitet.
Ich zaudre noch, die Kerzen auszublasen,
70 Nun hör ich sie, wie leise sie auch gleitet,
Mit giergem Blick die Hochgestalt umschweif ich,
Sie legt sich bei, die Wohlgestalt ergreif ich.

## X

Sie macht sich los: Vergönne, daß ich rede,
Damit ich dir nicht völlig fremd gehöre.
Der Schein ist wider mich; sonst war ich blöde,
Stets gegen Männer setzt ich mich zur Wehre.
Mich nennt die Stadt, mich nennt die Gegend spröde;
Nun aber weiß ich, wie das Herz sich kehre:
Du bist mein Sieger, laß dich's nicht verdrießen,
80 Ich sah, ich liebte, schwur dich zu genießen.

## XI

Du hast mich rein, und wenn ich's besser wüßte,
So gäb ich's dir, ich tue was ich sage.
So schließt sie mich an ihre süßen Brüste,
Als ob ihr nur an meiner Brust behage.
Und wie ich Mund und Aug und Stirne küßte,
So war ich doch in wunderbarer Lage:
Denn der so hitzig sonst den Meister spielet
Weicht schülerhaft zurück und abgekühlet.

## IX

Now midnight's here; streets, houses are at rest;
My bed is wide, but I have settled for
The narrowest share of it, at the behest
Of Love, that all-foreseeing counsellor.
My candles burn still, as with daintiest
Of footfalls she comes gliding to my door.          70
Her lovely form I seize with eager eyes
And then with eager arms, as down she lies.


## X

Still she withdraws: 'There's something I must tell
You, or we'll still be strangers! I know how
Things look to you, but please, try to think well
Of me. I've never gone with men till now;
They say I'm cold. I was a silly girl
Till I met you! But then I made a vow
That I would have you – yes, this very night!
You mustn't mind; I loved you at first sight,          80


## XI

And I am still a virgin – otherwise
I'd not pretend; I've told you all I know.'
She hugs me close to her sweet breasts, and lies
There in my arms, happy at last. But though
I kissed her now, her mouth, her brow, her eyes,
I was in wonderous quandary even so:
My master player, hitherto so hot,
Shrinks, novice-like, its ardour quite forgot.

## XII

Ihr scheint ein süßes Wort, ein Kuß zu gnügen,
90  Als wär es alles was ihr Herz begehrte.
Wie keusch sie mir, mit liebevollem Fügen,
Des süßen Körpers Fülleform gewährte!
Entzückt und froh in allen ihren Zügen
Und ruhig dann, als wenn sie nichts entbehrte.
So ruht ich auch, gefällig sie beschauend,
Noch auf den Meister hoffend und vertrauend.

## XIII

Doch als ich länger mein Geschick bedachte,
Von tausend Flüchen mir die Seele kochte,
Mich selbst verwünschend, grinsend mich belachte,
100  Nichts besser ward, wie ich auch zaudern mochte:
Da lag sie schlafend, schöner als sie wachte;
Die Lichter dämmerten mit langem Dochte.
Der Tages-Arbeit, jugendlicher Mühe
Gesellt sich gern der Schlaf und nie zu frühe.

## XIV

So lag sie himmlisch an bequemer Stelle,
Als wenn das Lager ihr allein gehörte,
Und an die Wand gedrückt, gequetscht zur Hölle,
Ohnmächtig Jener, dem sie nichts verwehrte.
Vom Schlangenbisse fällt zunächst der Quelle
110  Ein Wandrer so, den schon der Durst verzehrte.
Sie atmet lieblich holdem Traum entgegen;
Er hält den Atem, sie nicht aufzuregen.

## XII

How chaste she was! for though she made me free
Of her sweet body, loving words, a kiss                    90
Contented her; she nestled close to me,
Desiring, as it seemed, no more than this;
Happy she looked, peacefully, yieldingly
Satisfied, as if nothing were amiss.
So I too lay and watched her, glad of heart,
Still hoping, trusting in that master part.

## XIII

But as I further pondered my mischance
I raged a thousandfold, my soul was rent
With cursing and self-mockery both at once:
Wait as I might, there was no betterment.                   100
She slept, lovelier than waking innocence;
The candles flickered, their long wicks half-spent.
To youth, after a day's hard toil, the boon
Of willing slumber never comes too soon.

## XIV

So the dear angel lies, and as if all
The bed were hers, spreads each commodious limb,
While he, still powerless, squashed against the wall,
Must forfeit what she freely offered him.
Thus a parched wanderer still is doomed to fall
By snakebite at the fountain's very rim.                    110
She breathes in her sweet dreams, and for her sake
He holds his breath; she dreams and does not wake.

## XV

Gefaßt bei dem, was ihm noch nie begegnet,
Spricht er zu sich: So mußt du doch erfahren,
Warum der Bräutigam sich kreuzt und segnet,
Vor Nestelknüpfen scheu sich zu bewahren.
Weit lieber da, wo's Hellebarden regnet,
Als hier im Schimpf! So war es nicht vor Jahren,
Als deine Herrin dir zum ersten Male
120   Vors Auge trat im prachterhellten Saale.


## XVI

Da quoll dein Herz, da quollen deine Sinnen,
So daß der ganze Mensch entzückt sich regte.
Zum raschen Tanze trugst du sie von hinnen,
Die kaum der Arm und schon der Busen hegte,
Als wolltest du dir selbst sie abgewinnen;
Vervielfacht war, was sich für sie bewegte:
Verstand und Witz und alle Lebensgeister
Und rascher als die andern jener Meister.


## XVII

So immerfort wuchs Neigung und Begierde,
130   Brautleute wurden wir im frühen Jahre,
Sie selbst des Maien schönste Blum und Zierde;
Wie wuchs die Kraft zur Lust im jungen Paare!
Und als ich endlich sie zur Kirche führte:
Gesteh ich's nur, vor Priester und Altare,
Vor deinem Jammerkreuz, blutrünstger Christe,
Verzeih mir's Gott! es regte sich der Iste.

## XV

Resigned to this most novel accident
He muses ruefully: So now you know
Why bridegrooms cross themselves, and what is meant
By magic knots.* Better a bloody foe
In battle than this shame! How different
Things once were with you, when long years ago
You met your lady,* on that first of nights,
In that glad throng, under the festive lights!          120

## XVI

Oh then did not your soul and senses leap,
Was all of you not ecstasy at once?
Scarcely in your arms, already she was deep
Into your heart. Who clasped her in that dance
More jealously than you, as if to keep
Her even from yourself? Intelligence,
Wit, vital powers all doubled — but still faster
Was *its* increase, that little lord and master!

## XVII

Thus still they grew, desire and tenderness;
We were betrothed in spring, and she was more          130
Lovely than any maytime's bloom; ah yes,
How strong it waxed, our youthful passion's store!
And when at last we wed, I do confess,
Before that altar and that priest, before
Thy wretched bloodstained cross, *domine Christe,**
God pardon me! it stirred and rose, my *iste.**

## XVIII

Und ihr, der Brautnacht reiche Bettgehänge,
Ihr Pfühle, die sich uns so breit erstreckten,
Ihr Teppiche, die Lieb und Lustgedränge
140  Mit seidenweichen Fittichen bedeckten,
Ihr Käfigvögel, deren Zwitschersänge
Zu neuer Lust und nie zu früh uns weckten,
Ihr kanntet uns, von eurem Schutz umfriedet,
Teilnehmend sie, mich immer unermüdet.

## XIX

Und wie wir oft sodann im Raub genossen
Nach Buhlenart des Ehstands heilge Rechte,
Von reifer Saat umwogt, vom Rohr umschlossen,
An manchem Unort, wo ich's mich erfrechte,
Wir waren augenblicklich, unverdrossen
150  Und wiederholt bedient vom braven Knechte!
Verfluchter Knecht, wie unerwecklich liegst du!
Und deinen Herrn ums schönste Glück betrügst du.

## XX

Doch Meister Iste hat nun seine Grillen
Und läßt sich nicht befehlen noch verachten,
Auf einmal ist er da, und ganz im stillen
Erhebt er sich zu allen seinen Prachten.
So steht es nun dem Wandrer ganz zu Willen,
Nicht lechzend mehr am Quell zu übernachten.
Er neigt sich hin, er will die Schläfrin küssen,
160  Allein er stockt, er fühlt sich weggerissen.

112

## XVIII

And you, the bridal bed's rich furnishings,
You pillows soft and wide for nuptial nights,
You woven fabrics with your silk-soft wings
Sheltering our bliss, our urgent lovers' rites;          140
You little cage-birds whose first twitterings,
Never too soon, woke us to fresh delights –
You knew us well, you saw how that kind soul
Received me as I played my tireless role.

## XIX

And then how often too, with wanton passion,
We'd furtively enjoy our married state!
Down in the waving corn, in shameless fashion,
Among the reeds our love we'd consummate,
And that good slave would give us double ration
Of service every time, early or late.          150
Now, thrice-accursèd slave, limp, lifeless toy,
You cheat your master of his dearest joy!

## XX

But wise Sir Iste,* he has many a mood:
He'll not be bidden, he'll not be ignored.
For now, to his full, splendid magnitude,
He rears up quietly of his own accord;
Now sweet refreshment need not be eschewed,
Now the benighted wanderer's life's restored!
He turns to wake the maiden with a kiss –
But something checks him: what new scruple's this?  160

Wer hat zur Kraft ihn wieder aufgestählet,
Als jenes Bild, das ihm auf ewig teuer,
Mit dem er sich in Jugendlust vermählet?
Dort leuchtet her ein frisch erquicklich Feuer,
Und wie er erst in Ohnmacht sich gequälet,
So wird nun hier dem Starken nicht geheuer.
Er schaudert weg, vorsichtig, leise, leise
Entzieht er sich dem holden Zauberkreise,

## XXII

Sitzt, schreibt: Ich nahte mich der heimschen Pforte,
170   Entfernen wollten mich die letzten Stunden,
Da hab ich nun, am sonderbarsten Orte,
Mein treues Herz aufs neue Dir verbunden.
Zum Schlusse findest du geheime Worte:
*Die Krankheit erst bewähret den Gesunden.*
Dies Büchlein soll dir manches Gute zeigen,
Das Beste nur muß ich zuletzt verschweigen.

## XXIII

Da kräht der Hahn. Das Mädchen schnell entwindet
Der Decke sich und wirft sich rasch ins Mieder.
Und da sie sich so seltsam wiederfindet,
180   So stutzt sie, blickt und schlägt die Augen nieder –
Und da sie ihm zum letzten Mal verschwindet,
Im Auge bleiben ihm die schönen Glieder.
Das Posthorn tönt, er wirft sich in den Wagen
Und läßt getrost sich zu der Liebsten tragen.

## XXI

What (he reflects) has steeled his strength again
But *her* dear image, whom he took to wife
In lusty youth? He loves her, now as then;
From her it glows, this freshening fire of life.
So his new vigour troubles him – as when
He lay here helpless, he's once more in strife
Of mind. A certain dread now gives him pause;
From the charmed circle gently he withdraws,


## XXII

Sits, writes: 'Nearing my homeward journey's end,
These last hours threatened distance and delay,          170
But my heart's true to you once more, dear friend,
And binds me to you in the strangest way.
Here some mysterious words I shall append:
*Sickness is the true proof of health*, they say.
This book shall tell you many a good thing,
But must not mention the best news I bring.'


## XXIII

Now the cock crows. Quickly the girl leaps out
Of bed, throws on her clothes; waking in these
Strange circumstances, she's confused no doubt,
Looks up, and then looks down again. Now he's          180
Bidding goodbye to her; she turns about,
And as she leaves, her shapely limbs still please
His eye. The carriage waits, the posthorn's sound
Cheers him, he's soon homeward and wifeward bound.

Und weil zuletzt bei jeder Dichtungsweise
Moralien uns ernstlich fördern sollen,
So will auch ich in so beliebtem Gleise
Euch gern bekennen, was die Verse wollen:
Wir stolpern wohl auf unsrer Lebensreise,
190   Und doch vermögen in der Welt, der tollen,
Zwei Hebel viel aufs irdische Getriebe:
Sehr viel die Pflicht, unendlich mehr die Liebe.

## XXIV*

But since the end of all poetic art
Is the improvement of the reader's mind
(Or so we're told), my verses for their part
Shall point the usual moral of their kind
And say: Our life's a road on which the heart
May stumble, yet two mighty powers we find          190
In this mad world to help us as we go:
To Duty much, to Love far more we owe.

# TRANSLATOR'S POSTSCRIPT

The English accentual elegiac metre of the present version of the *Roman Elegies* is intended to approximate to Goethe's German accentual elegiacs, which in their turn are no more than an approximation to the quantitative elegiacs of classical Greek and Latin. In ancient 'quantitative' verse the syllables are either 'long' (−) or 'short' (˘), whereas in Goethe's as in all other modern imitations this distinction is simply equated with that between stressed (/) and unstressed (×) syllables, although in fact it is a matter of controversy how quantity was related to stress in the ancient languages. But subject to this fundamental difference and given this interpretation of the model, Goethe follows it with reasonable strictness. The conventions which he evidently felt to be essential if a minimal sense of the specific 'elegiac' metre was to be retained, may be listed as follows:

(1) The verse is invariably in distichs (two-line units) each consisting of a hexameter followed by a pentameter.

(2) The hexameter contains neither more nor less than six 'feet', each of which (with certain exceptions as specified below) may be either a dactyl (− ˘ ˘, / × × ) or a spondee (− −, / / ).

(3) The sixth foot of the hexameter always has only two syllables and is thus never a dactyl. In Greek or Latin its second syllable was either long (making it a spondee) or short (making it in effect a trochee, − ˘, though some theorists describe this as a catalectic dactyl). In modern accentual imitations the so-called spondee in any case constantly tends to degenerate into a trochee, the latter rhythm ( / × ) being therefore much the commoner one in disyllabic feet, whether at the end of the hexameter or elsewhere.

(4) The penultimate foot of the hexameter must be a dactyl, i.e. the hexameter ends / × × / (/), not / / / (/).

(5) The pentameter has a fixed central 'caesura' or (at least notional) break, which divides it symmetrically into two half-lines (hemistichs) each of two-and-a-half feet, the last syllable of each hemistich therefore being always 'long' (stressed).

(6) In no case does any line, or the second hemistich of any pentameter, begin with an unstressed syllable (anacrusis).

(7) The second hemistich of the pentameter must contain two dactyls, i.e. it is always / ˣ ˣ / ˣ ˣ / .

In some other respects, however, Goethe treats the theoretical metrical requirements with a certain nonchalance, quite rightly compromising between them and the natural rhythms of speech. He resisted the attempts of learned friends to correct the prosody of his lines, preferring, even when he had sought their advice, to rely in the end on his own ear. His unstressed syllables, for instance, are often very 'incorrect' if thought of as the equivalent of 'short' syllables: thus the second syllable of 'Theseus' (XV, 332f.), especially as pronounced in German, does not work well as the first short of a dactyl, and an extreme case is 'und Violettstrumpf dazu' (VIII, 172): in the second dactyl of this phrase, 'strumpf' is supposed to be a short though its vowel is sandwiched between two groups of four consonants. There was also the vexed question of whether the German hexameter, like the pentameter, must or could contain a caesura, and if so where; by ancient theory it was supposed to, with permitted variations of position. Goethe seems to have largely left this point to take care of itself, and in practice his at least notional hexameter-caesura usually falls as a natural enough break after the first or (if it is a dactyl) second syllable of the third foot. In general, he evidently found that this ancient and formal metre could be made to work informally and with its conventions lightly worn.

Goethe's purpose was to write erotic poetry in stylized classical verse, and the elegiac distich suited him admirably: he had discovered in it a law which paradoxically served his liberating project and made a new stylistic synthesis possible. As the late Emil Staiger pointed out in his masterly study,* a verse-form regulated in certain ways, but requiring no rhyme, was one in which he could obey rules while virtually improvising. It may be significant, as Staiger suggests, that Goethe always avoided the appreciably more difficult four-line strophic forms of ancient poetry, much as he admired Horace and Catullus and their other great practitioners. Could the balance between liberty and convention have been preserved, could the syllables of alcaics or asclepiads have been counted out with his fingers on his sleeping mistress's back, as he tells us his hexameters were (VII, 149f.)? He

* *Goethe*, Atlantis Verlag, Zürich, 1956, vol. 2, pp. 66f.

never seems to have tried it; but hexameters and pentameters he used with fluency and relish for many years. He delighted, for instance, in the neat devices of antithesis and chiasmus to which the distich and especially the symmetrical pentameter lend themselves (as in VII, 140 and 144; 'Werd ich auch halb nur gelehrt, bin ich doch doppelt beglückt . . .', 'Sehe mit fühlendem Aug, fühle mit sehender Hand . . .'). As Goethe well knew, such felicities are directly inspired by the metrical rule which he had embraced.

If this urbane, ironic and unpompous flavour of informality within a formal convention is to be appreciated, anyone reading the *Elegies* aurally or aloud must adopt a reasonably tactful and flexible interpretation of the relative stresses and speeds within the lines. The same is meant to apply to the present English version, which seeks to retain something of the original's characteristic qualities by fairly closely observing most of the 'minimum' rules of elegiacs listed above, while not attempting to be less liberal about them than Goethe was. For example I have tried throughout to retain the essential fixed caesura of the pentameter or at least to suggest its pattern of two hemistichs even when there is in practice no appreciable break between them. In VII, 144 the pentameter 'Seeing with vision that feels, feeling with fingers that see' clearly shows its symmetrical structure, which the natural speech-rhythm supports; in VII, 146 on the other hand ('Hours of night as a rich recompense she can bestow') the required stress and caesura are notional rather than actual, though 'rich recompense' should be read in such a way as not to destroy them altogether. In English, appropriate scansions can often be unobtrusively suggested by an accommodating enunciation of the words, mainly because so many English vowels are diphthongal or triphthongal: thus 'hours' in the line just quoted may be read disyllabically (making 'hours of' a suggested dactyl). Similar treatment is invited by pentameter-endings which would otherwise be too spondaic (rule 7), such as 'with corn-ears wreathed' in XIV, 266 and 'encircling arm' in XV, 320; and on the same principle, a word such as 'tedious' or 'odious' occurring as the last foot of a hexameter would be read as having not three syllables but two (rule 3).

The required scansion of lines is generally obvious in Latin or Greek or even German, but less so in English, in which the predominance of monosyllabic words makes for metrical ambiguity. Unless the obtrusive device of written stress accents is adopted it becomes difficult, merely by the speech-rhythms of English, to guide the reader in the right prosodic direction. The language's lack of inflection and therefore comparatively rigid word-order is a further problem. Nevertheless it is not true, though often asserted, that English accentual hexameters and pentameters must inevitably sound unnatural or faintly ridiculous, and that in order to produce a tolerable English equivalent of such lines their prosodic basis must be virtually abandoned. I have sought to avoid lending colour to this comfortable theory, which was in any case disproved by W. H. Auden in his poem 'Natural Linguistics' (1969), an effortless metrical analogue of correct elegiacs and a model example of the kind of equivalent I am here attempting.

In the *Roman Elegies*, a still relatively young poet in his first 'classical' years was for the first time deliberately attaching himself to a stylistic tradition centuries old, and finding that its yoke was easy and its burden light. In *Das Tagebuch*, written about twenty years later, the long-since mature master was setting himself, and accomplishing with sovereign ease, an even more sophisticated metrical task. The significance of Goethe's choice for this poem of the *ottava rima* stanza, a metre he infrequently used, has already been discussed in the Introduction. Another example of it is the opening 'Dedication' in *Faust*. The prosodic conventions of *ottava rima* are clearer than those of elegiac verse and probably less unfamiliar to most modern readers. An Italian invention like so many forms of rhymed verse, it was brought to perfection and great prominence as the established metre of the high Renaissance epic (Ariosto and Tasso in Italy, Camões in Portugal). Its unvarying scheme of eight iambic five-foot lines rhyming ab ab ab cc presents no great difficulty in the Romance languages, but in German and especially in English, with fewer rhyming words to choose from, the problem is harder to solve. Moreover, a strict imitation of the Italian norm of hendecasyllabic lines would require the rhymes to be 'feminine' throughout. This is essentially alien to English verse, and in practice masculine rhyming has been allowed to predominate in English imitations of *ottava rima*, as well as in its slightly more elaborate variant the Spenserian stanza. It is significant that the major English example of the form, Byron's satirical epic *Don Juan*, uses feminine rhymes as lavishly and as ingeniously as possible, but that the effect is usually one of deliberately facetious self-parody. In German the difficulty is less acute, and thanks largely to Goethe a compromise was achieved: in every case of his use of the *ottava* metre, except one, he adopted a strict alternation of feminine and masculine rhymes (i.e. of hendecasyllabic and decasyllabic lines), and this established itself as the standard German practice.

The single exception was *Das Tagebuch*, one of the remarkable features of which is that throughout its twenty-four stanzas the rhymes are feminine, the Italian hendecasyllabic model is followed exactly. It is rather as if Goethe had reserved for this poem, which he knew he could never publish, the same virtuosity as he was to show in his only two excursions into the even more exacting metre of *terza rima*, the linking ternary form (aba bcb cdc ded, etc.) made famous by Dante. Late in 1826, in his seventy-eighth year, a new German translation of the *Divine Comedy* inspired him to write the solemn meditation 'On Contemplating Schiller's Skull' and Faust's splendid speech greeting the sunrise at the beginning of *Faust Part Two*, both of which not only follow Dante's rhyme-scheme but are also hendecasyllabic throughout. The *ottava rima* of *Das Tagebuch* is ultra-strict in the same way, and in translating it I should greatly have liked to be able to imitate this, as a distinctive element in the poem's specific character. But just as there are fewer feminine rhymes in German than in Italian, so also there are far fewer in English than in German; German has therefore always been able to make much greater use of hendecasyllables and in general to follow more demanding conventions. (Stefan George's fastidiously hendecasyllabic translation of selections from Dante in 1909 is another outstanding example.) In English, when the *ottava* or *terza* rhyme-scheme has been adopted at all (as in the classic translations of Ariosto and Tasso or some versions of Dante), the hendecasyllabic observance seems always to have been regarded as impossible, or in any case at variance with the spirit of the language. I regretfully decided that it would also be impossible here, even in a shorter poem and notwithstanding such translator's licences as overrunning and paraphrase; accordingly I have conformed to the English tradition and imitated Goethe's feminine endings only in a minority of cases.

# EXPLANATORY NOTES

## ROMAN ELEGIES

I: The significance of the two hitherto suppressed 'priapic' Elegies I and XXIV is explained and discussed in the Introduction. Both are modelled on the Latin *Carmina Priapea*, the first-century collection of epigrams in honour of Priapus which Goethe had studied at the time of writing the *Roman Elegies*, and it is evident that he originally conceived them as prologue and epilogue to the cycle. Priapus (stressed on the second syllable in Latin, German and English) was a fertility-god whose cult spread from Asia Minor to Greece in Hellenistic times; according to the Greeks his parents were the wine-god Dionysos (Bacchus) and the love-goddess Aphrodite (Venus) (cf. Elegy XIII). The Romans adopted him as a god of gardens, in which his comically phallic statue would be set up as a kind of combined scarecrow (cf. Elegy XIX) and tutelary deity. (He survives today as the sentimentalized and of course de-phallicized 'garden gnome'.) In Elegies I and XXIV Goethe takes over and develops some of the stock motifs of the *Priapea*, notably the conventional symbolic parallel between a book and a garden, poems and the fruit which Priapus is appointed to guard (cf. *Priapea*, II, LX, etc., op. cit., Introduction, note 22), and the phallic penalties (ibid., XXII, XXIV, LXXII, etc.) which the guardian will inflict on unwanted intruders. Thus in the first Elegy Goethe introduces his cycle of erotic verse as a 'garden of love', neatly divided into separate flowerbeds (elegies) and watched over by the god, and the 'marauders' as hypocritical readers who will be offended (cf. *Priapea*, XLIX) by these poems which are 'fruits of pure Nature'; they are accordingly threatened with an 'unnatural' sexual assault.

For the 1815 edition (which did not contain Elegies, I, III, XVII and XXIV) Goethe added a two-line rhymed epigraph:

> Wie wir einst so glücklich waren!
> Müssens erst durch euch erfahren.

> We were happy once; and now
> Let my verse remind us how.

I, 1: *flowers of Eros*: on the translation of 'Liebe' cf. note on III, 29.

II, 11: *Genius, how idly you sleep*: this hemistich has usually been understood as an invocation of the *genius loci* (translatable therefore as: 'Spirit of Rome, are you dumb?') As suggested in the Introduction, however, it is in the present context probably an invocation of Priapus. It may be, of course, that Goethe is ironically equating the two.

III, 29: *Eros*: constant reference to the personification of sexual love ('amor') was part of the Latin stylistic convention which Goethe is imitating. He consistently calls the love-god either simply 'Liebe' or uses, as here, his Latin name 'Amor' (scanned in German as a trochee); in the *Elegies* generally, however, he does not exclude the Greek names for the gods ('Zeus' appearing occasionally for Jupiter and 'Hermes' regularly replacing Mercury). 'Cupid' would be a correct English translation of 'Amor', but I have preferred 'Eros' (with the anglicized pronunciation) as being also trochaic but slightly more flexible.

III, 37f.: *Princess Borghese . . . Nipotina*: well-known Roman beauties of more recent times, married respectively to Prince Marcantonio Borghese and to the papal nepote Count Braschi.

IV, 57–64: *Now at last . . .*: the first four distichs of this elegy originally read:

Fraget nun, wen ihr auch wollt, mich werdet ihr nimmer erreichen,
　Schöne Damen, und ihr, Herren der feineren Welt!
Ob denn auch Werther gelebt? Ob denn auch alles fein wahr sei?
　Welche Stadt sich mit Recht Lottens, der einzigen, rühmt?
Ach, wie hab ich so oft die törichten Blätter verwünschet,
　Die mein jugendlich Leid unter die Menge gebracht!
Wäre Werther mein Bruder gewesen, ich hätt ihn erschlagen,
　Kaum verfolgte mich so rächend sein trauriger Geist . . .

Now at last I am safe from you all! Go elsewhere with your questions,
　My fair ladies, my fine gentlemen of the *beau monde*!
Was there really a Werther? and is the book the true story?
　In which town did the dear Lotte in fact really live?
Foolish pages! alas, how often I've cursed you: you spread my
　Youthful sorrow abroad, made it the talk of the world!
Even if Werther had been my brother and if I had killed him –
　I'd have been scarcely so plagued by his avenging sad ghost! . . .

Goethe later altered these revealingly personal lines, which allude to the simplistic popular view of him as above all else the author of *The Sorrows of Young Werther* (1774). By the time of the *Elegies* he had outgrown the romantic sensibility of his youthful novel, the fame of which caused him life-long embarrassment.

IV, 65–9: *Malbrouk*: a satirical song about the Duke of Marlborough, beginning 'Malbrouk s'en va-t-en guerre . . .', was in the 1780s tediously popular all over Europe.

IV, 70, 74: *the mob . . . folly of kings . . . Gallic frenzy*: alluding to the French Revolution.

V, 93: *Anchises*: the Trojan prince whom Venus took as her lover, and who thus became the father of the hero Aeneas.

V, 95: *Endymion*: a shepherd boy, loved by Diana.

V, 97: *Leander*: the young man from Abydos who fell in love with Hero, the priestess of Aphrodite at Sestos, and swam every night to her across the Hellespont, finally perishing in a storm.

V, 99: *Rhea Sylvia*: a Vestal virgin seduced by Mars; their children Romulus and Remus were exposed to starve but were suckled by a she-wolf and lived to become the legendary founders of Rome.

VI, 117: *whirled on a wheel or chained to a cliff-face*: alluding to the fates of Ixion (who had tried to seduce Juno) and of Prometheus (who had stolen the secret of fire from the gods to give it to men).

VI, 121: *Proteus, Thetis*: a sea-god and sea-goddess noted for their ability to transform themselves into various shapes.

VI, 127: *thus she appeared to me*: Goethe may be alluding to his first meeting with Christiane-'Faustina' and to her attractive hairstyle, which figures prominently in his drawings of her (cf. the reproductions of these in the studies mentioned in note 16 to the Introduction). The passage also echoes late Roman allegorical descriptions of the 'goddess Opportunity' as wearing her hair short behind and long in front, to encourage men to seize her (as we still say) 'by the forelock'.

VII, 137f.: *counsels . . . of the ancients*: probably alluding to the advice of Horace to his readers (*De arte poetica*, 268f.):

> vos exemplaria Graeca
> nocturna versate manu, versate diurna.

> Let the works of the Greeks be
> Held in your hands each day, each night let your hands
> still explore them.

VII, 154: *Triumvirs, three poets of love*: Goethe's acknowledged models for the *Elegies* were the Latin erotic poets Gaius Valerius Catullus (ca. 84–54 BC), Albius Tibullus (ca. 48–19 BC), and Sextus Propertius (ca. 48–15 BC). The Renaissance philologist Scaliger called them the 'triumviri amoris'.

VIII, 160, 182: *the husband I lost . . . her little boy*: 'Faustina' is a widow with a young child. It is interesting in this connection that on his return from Italy in 1788 Goethe is reported as telling his Weimar friends that 'in Rome there is no debauchery with unmarried women, but it is all the more customary with the married ones' (letter from Schiller to Körner, 7 September 1788). A young widow would presumably have been an even better choice, and this lends plausibility to the status here apparently ascribed to the poet's fictionalized mistress, given the inaccessibility of virgins and the risk of venereal disease with prostitutes (cf. XVII and XXI).

VIII, 168f.: *Falconieri, Albani*: names of well-known Roman families; it is uncertain, and immaterial, whether any allusion to specific persons is intended.

VIII, 172: *scarlet and purple*: the colours of gaiters worn by cardinals and bishops.

VIII, 182 *see* note to l. 160.

IX, 192: *wearisome world*: the original version of the elegy contains at this point the following additional distich:

> Da ein trauriges Bette dem darbenden Armen vergebens
> Lohn der einsamen Nacht, ruhige Stunden, verhieß . . .

> Poor frustrated wretch! through those lonely nights on my cheerless
> Bed I would vainly await sleep as their only reward.

IX, 202, 209: *guest-honouring Jove . . . god of hospitality*: among the numerous epithets of Zeus was 'xenios', indicating that the relationship between host and guest was sacred to him; the Romans correspondingly called him 'Jupiter hospes' or 'hospitalis'.

IX, 203: *goddess of Youth*: Hebe, who welcomed Hercules to Olympus.

IX, 209 *see* note to l. 202.

IX, 213: *Hermes*: the reference to Hermes (Mercury) here concerns his function as the god who guided the souls of the dead to the underworld (but cf. XVII).

IX, 214: *Cestius' tomb*: the so-called Pyramid of Cestius beside the Protestant cemetery. Goethe is on record as having imagined during his stay in Rome that he might die there and be buried in its shadow; his son August was in fact buried in this cemetery in 1830.

XII, 231: *Henry and Frederick*: Henri IV of France (1553–1610), and (probably) Friedrich II of Prussia ('Frederick the Great', 1712–86) who had recently died.

XIII: This elegy, placed at a central point in the cycle, is closely related to I and XXIV in that all three are in honour of Priapus (cf. Introduction), though XIII expresses this homage in a disguised and contrived manner whereas the other two do so more openly. In XIII the poet implicitly compares himself to a sculptor, as in XXIV. A sculptor's workshop is like a pantheon of deities, and among them are Bacchus (Dionysos) and Venus (Aphrodite, Cythere), the parents of the phallic god whose statue they miss; the artist will respond by supplying one. Similarly, the poet writes erotic elegies which celebrate sensuous joy, and which can take their rightful place among other and more solemn poetic forms. Having thus artistically rehabilitated the erotic principle, he lays his poems on the altar of the Graces in gratitude for their favour.

XIV, 249: *Via Flaminia*: Goethe's lodging in Rome was near the Porto del Popolo, from which the Via Flaminia runs northwards into the Campagna.

XIV, 252: *Ceres*: the Roman name for Demeter, the goddess of agriculture; before being enlightened by her, men subsisted not on corn or other 'cereals', but on more primitive nourishment such as acorns.

XIV, 258: *Eleusis*: the place near Athens at which the 'Eleusinian Mysteries' were celebrated for many centuries. Demeter had supposedly lived for some time at Eleusis and on her departure founded these orgiastic rites, which also honoured the god Dionysos (Bacchus) and Demeter's daughter Persephone (Proserpina). The Romans did not fully adopt this cult until the time of the Emperor Hadrian, when Greece had long been a province under the Roman conquest.

XIV, 273: *Jasion*: scanned here as a dactyl, though strictly it should be stressed on the last syllable. The association of this particular amour of Demeter's (of which an account is given by Ovid) with the Eleusinian festival is an invention by Goethe.

XV, 315: *friend of the Muses*: proverbially, 'Aurora' is 'Musis amica'.

XV, 321f.: *could the quiet hours preserve you*: it is not clear whether 'erhieltet' is to be read as a past indicative or as a past subjunctive, though either one or the other, but not both, must be intended. In the latter case (past subjunctive conditional) the sense would be: 'what a joyful awakening (it would be) if the quiet hours could preserve for me a memorial of the pleasure that rocked us to sleep' – that is, if he were to find that the experience could be turned into a poem. This is the usual interpretation, in keeping with the theme central to this Elegy and prominent in the cycle as a whole (cf. II, VII, XXIII), namely that of the relationship between love and art, in particular the poet's ironically conceived problem about whether to spend his time making love or in writing and study, and his solution to this dilemma by composing poetry while in bed with 'Faustina' (VII). If on the other hand 'erhieltet' is a past indicative, then the sense is: 'what a joyful awakening (it is) when' (or 'if') 'the quiet hours have preserved a memorial . . .', etc. In this case, although Goethe might still be saying that he is delighted when he wakes up finding in his mind the inception of a new poem about the past night's love-making, it would be equally in keeping with the spirit of the *Elegies* if he meant that he is delighted to find himself (after restful sleep and perhaps some quiet contemplation of his still sleeping companion) as sexually potent as before, i.e. the 'memorial' or 'monument' is his erect penis. This meaning would fully bring together the twin themes of sexual potency and artistic creativity, and would closely link the present Elegy to *The Diary* (cf. Introduction) as well as to I and XXIV. It would also lend plausibility to Thomas Mann's imaginative reconstruction of the poet's later life in his novel *Lotte in Weimar*, chapter VII of which introduces the elderly Goethe with a *monologue intérieur* as he wakes in the early morning: his first thoughts are of an erotic dream to the bodily 'monument' of which he addresses congratulatory remarks. In translating this distich of XV I have tried to devise a rendering that would accommodate the different possible readings here considered.

XV, 332: *Ariadne*: one of the daughters of King Minos of Crete, who helped the hero Theseus to kill the Minotaur in its labyrinth; he then abducted her, but abandoned her as she lay asleep on the island of Naxos, where Bacchus later found and consoled her.

XVII, 343: *Python*: the dragon killed by Apollo at Delphi.

XVII, 343: *Hydra*: another monster, with nine heads and living in a swamp at Lerna; it was killed by the hero Hercules (cf. XXII) as one of his Twelve Labours.

XVII, 348: *new monster*: Goethe makes the traditional assumption that venereal disease was unknown in Europe before medieval times; in the absence of evidence to the contrary this view is still generally accepted.

XVII, 351: *Hesperian dragon*: the serpent Ladon which kept watch over the tree of golden apples in the garden of the 'daughters of the west' (Hesperides).

XVII, 357: *Lucretius*: Titus Lucretius Carus (d. 55 BC), author of the didactic epic *De rerum natura*, in which he recommends sexual promiscuity (IV, 1063–72).

XVII, 359: *Propertius*: cf. note on VII, 154; 'Cynthia' was the fictional name of his mistress.

XVII, 370: *Semele*: the mother of Bacchus by Jupiter, who destroyed her by appearing to her in his true form as the god of thunder and lightning.

XVII, 370: *Callisto*: another of Jupiter's mistresses, whom he concealed by turning her into a she-bear, and later raised to the heavens as a constellation.

XVII, 373: *Juno*: the wife of Jupiter, always jealous of his infidelities (see also XXII).

XVII, 378: *Mercury knows the cure*: derivatives of mercury (quicksilver) were in the eighteenth century widely believed to be effective for the treatment of syphilis.

XVIII, 389–9: *Caesar, Florus*: according to Hadrian's biographer Spartian, the poet Florus had composed an epigram to the effect that he would not wish to be the Emperor, engaged in arduous travel and military expeditions which even exposed him to the British climate; Hadrian had replied in a counter-epigram that he would not change his lot for that of Florus who spends his time in low Roman taverns and eating-houses being bitten by fleas.

XVIII, 394: *osterie*: wine-taverns, the word being 'fittingly' derived from *oste* (landlord); cf. the English 'hostelry'.

XVIII, 395: *her uncle*: the Latin poets commonly assign to an uncle (*patruus*) the role of watching over and censuring the morals of his nephews and nieces (see also XIX).

XVIII, 403: *over the table it spilled*: the theme of assignations or other amorous messages written surreptitiously in wine on the table-top was common in the Latin poets. Ovid for instance writes in the *Heroides* (xvii, 87):

> orbe quoque in mensae legi sub nomine nostro
> quod deducta mero littera fecit AMO.

> And what is more, on the round table-top where you'd
> written my name out
> In the wine, you would add letters composing I LOVE.

and in the *Ars amatoria* (i, 571f.):

> Blanditiasque leves tenui perscribere vino
> Ut dominam in mensa se legat illa tuam.

> And in a film of wine you may write some affectionate message,
> So on the table she'll read she is the lady you love.

Cf. also *Amores* i 4,20 and ii 5,17, likewise Tibullus i 6,18f. and Propertius iii 8,25.

XVIII, 410: *'IV'*: the assignation is made for 'four' o'clock according to the old system of time-keeping which (as Goethe notes in his *Italian Journey*) was still in use in eighteenth-century Rome, i.e. for the fourth hour after nightfall.

XVIII, 416: *Horace foretold*: Horace (*Carmen saeculare* 11f.) declares that the sun will never have seen anything greater than the city of Rome.

XVIII, 428: *fortunate robbers*: probably alluding to the legend of how Romulus's men, at the time of the foundation of Rome, forcibly carried off the women of the neighbouring Sabine tribe.

XIX: This elegy again introduces the theme of the watchful uncle (cf. XVII), as well as that of the scarecrow and the sexual symbolism of the garden (cf. I, XXIV).

XXI, 464: *serpents and poison*: Goethe reverts here to the theme of venereal disease developed in XVII.

XXII, 480: *Reputation*: 'Fama' (the word literally means spoken report, rumour, hence also repute, reputation, fame) was personified as a malignant and unpleasant goddess by Latin poets, notably by Vergil (*Aeneid* iv, 173–97, where she spreads abroad the amour of Dido and Aeneas); Ovid also describes her as living in a 'brazen' tower (*Metamorphoses* xii, 39–63). Goethe's story of her feud with Cupid is an inventive recombination of various classical motifs.

XXII, 488, 491: *Hercules, Alcmene*: the demigod Hercules was born to Alcmene, wife of the Theban general Amphitryon, after Jupiter had seduced her by impersonating her husband.

XXII, 488: *Hercules now is my slave*: i.e. he is now concerned only with fame and self-glorification.

XXII, 491 *see* note to l. 488.

XXII, 499: *the Amazon's victor*: one of the Twelve Labours of Hercules was to rob the Amazon queen Hippolyta of her girdle.

XXII, 504: *a fair lady*: requiring healing and purification after his great deeds, Hercules was told by the Delphic oracle that he must sell himself into servitude for three years; accordingly he became a slave of Omphale, queen of Lydia. During this time Omphale is said to have amused herself by wearing the hero's lion-skin costume, and he by dressing up as a woman and using a spinning-wheel. Descendants of Hercules later became kings of Lydia.

XXII, 521: *Vulcan*: in the story told by Homer the god Vulcan, a skilled metalsmith, invented a booby-trapped bed to catch his wife Venus with her lover Mars, to the vast amusement of the other gods. Goethe had always relished this famous episode (*Odyssey* vii, 267–343), and had alluded to it in an interesting symbolic way in one of his early Storm and Stress poems (see the analysis of 'Künstlers Morgenlied' by Hans Rudolf Vaget, 'Eros und Apoll', in *Jahrbuch der Schillergesellschaft*, XXX, 1986).

XXII, 547f.: *the old rule . . . the Greeks paid for it*: quoting Horace's comment (*Epistolae* i, 2,14) on the Trojan war as recounted in Homer's *Iliad* ('quidquid delirant reges, plectuntur Achivi').

XXIII, 556: *Midas*: Ovid (*Metamorphoses* xi, 174–93) tells the story of how King Midas of Phrygia, for criticizing Apollo's musicianship, had his ears changed into those of an ass. He was able to conceal them from everyone except his barber, but the latter, as a compromise with the oath of silence that burdened him, eventually dug a hole in the earth and whispered the secret into it, whereupon reeds grew up at this spot and murmured into the wind, the matter thus becoming public knowledge.

XXIV: The cycle closes with the second of the two openly 'Priapic' elegies (cf. I and Introduction). In this epilogue Priapus himself speaks, to thank the poet for rehabilitating him (as his parents Bacchus and Venus had wished in XIII). Now that the *Roman Elegies* have been written, he is no longer a dilapidated old wooden image in a forgotten and neglected garden: 'the artist' has made him a smart new statue of more durable material (line 14), and honoured by all and sundry. In gratitude, the god now blesses the poet's sexual prowess (which on another level, as in *The Diary*, also represents his creative power).

XXIV, 602: *Philaenis*: a courtesan to whom the authorship of a well-known ancient erotic manual was attributed. The phrase, coming significantly in this final distich of the *Roman Elegies*, is a direct quotation from the *Priapea* (no. LXIII): 'tot figurae, quot Philaenis enarrat', i.e. as many sexual positions as she describes.

## THE DIARY

(title:) in both the surviving MSS (see Introduction) the date '1810' immediately follows the word *'Tagebuch'*, which may mean that Goethe intended this to be part of the title itself (*The Diary 1810*, or *The 1810 Diary*).

(epigraph:) from Tibullus (i 5, 39f.). The Latin distich in fact begins 'Saepe aliam tenui . . .', giving the sense: '(Often) I held another woman in my arms, but as I was about to take my pleasure Venus reminded me of my lady and deserted me.' Goethe omits the first word and disregards the context of the lines, thus adapting them to the situation in his own poem, of which they are an integral and highly important component.

116: *magic knots*: the spells (usually involving the symbolic tying of a knot) by which loving or jealous women were thought to render men impotent with any other partner.

119: *lady (Herrin)*: i.e. his future wife (cf. the 'domina' of the Tibullus epigraph).

135: the German text literally reads 'before thy wretched cross, bloodstained Christ . . .' Goethe originally seems to have written 'blutströmig', then 'blutstriemig', finally adopting 'blutrünstig'; all these mean 'running with blood' (from wounds, etc.) though 'blutrünstig' in twentieth century use has come to mean 'bloodthirsty'. Goethe's provocative combination of this line with the next, though thematically central to the whole poem, has always been found particularly offensive, so that in nearly all the earlier printings of *Das Tagebuch* lines 135f. are editorially reworded or partly excised (cf. Introduction).

136: Goethe's choice of the Latin pronoun 'iste' (= that, this) to denote the penis is discussed in the Introduction. So far as its precise Latin meaning is concerned, 'iste' has been called the 'demonstrative of the second person' because it was chiefly (but by no means exclusively) used to refer to something near or belonging or related to, or otherwise associated with, the person addressed ('that thing of yours', 'that of which you speak', etc.). The second-person element however is often notional or virtually absent, the reference being merely to persons or things of which the hearer is aware ('that . . . which you have heard of', 'the well-known . . .'; cf. in German 'das bewußte . . .'). The 'iste' forms also frequently carried a derogatory or contemptuous nuance: 'isti' 'these persons', 'iste' 'that fellow' (whom we are discussing), 'iste insolens barbarus' ('that insolent savage'). A usage that comes close to Goethe's occurs in the *Priapea* (no. LVI), when the god addresses an intruder to the garden with a threatening reference to his own displayed phallus (cf. Elegy I) which he calls simply 'ista', with the feminine noun *'mentula'* (the obscene word for penis) understood, i.e. 'this (prick which you see)'; the same euphemistic use of the first person possessive 'mea' by itself (for 'mea mentula') is also found. Goethe's 'der Iste' is thus (the narrator addressing the reader) 'this thing of mine (which I am telling you about)'; the definite article 'der' is in the context equivalent to 'my', as commonly in German. One might indeed say that all three grammatical persons are here implicitly present: the *I* to whom the recalcitrant organ belongs, the *you* to *whom* the poet has been describing its behaviour, and the thing *itself* from which he is now so ruefully dissociated. It is not clear whether 'Iste' and (line 153) 'Meister Iste' in Goethe's sense are entirely his own coinage in German, though this seems probable.

153: *wise Sir Iste*: I have here avoided the straightforward rendering of 'Meister Iste' as 'Master Iste' because of the intrusive English connotation, in this case, of 'Master' in the sense of an under-age boy (as in Master John, Master Smith, etc., or Dickens's homophonous 'Master Bates'). The German 'Meister', here and in lines 87, 96 and 128, suggests the mature master of a skill as distinct from a novice, a learned master performer, as well as perhaps some kind of honorific title.

185–92: the ironies and ambiguities of the closing stanza are discussed in the Introduction. For translation purposes I have assumed the following interpretations: (a) 'stolpern' (stumble) refers to the narrator's near-adultery (paralleling the daemonic temptation of the first stanza, line 7), and not, as has sometimes been thought, to his temporary impotence; (b) the statement 'zwei Hebel vermögen viel', i.e. two forces (literally 'two levers') can do much, means not that the two forces (duty and love) are in conflict but that they are both our allies, though one is greater than the other (paralleling 'so waltet was . . .' in line 8, i.e., literally, 'something prevails' and 'saves our virtue'); (c) 'die Pflicht' (duty) is in this context the narrator's (or our) 'plighted troth', his marital duty to be faithful to his wife and potent with her; and (d) 'die Liebe' is the deep sexual passion which not only drives him into the arms of a stranger, but is also – and chiefly – directed towards his wife, as a personal love which binds his potency to her as if with a 'magic knot'. It is thus a greater power than duty, and transcends morality only to reinforce it in an ironic and unexpected way.

# INDEX TO ROMAN ELEGIES

The renumbering of the Elegies adopted in the present edition is given below, with the traditional numbering of the corresponding poems added in brackets. **I and XXIV were omitted in all previous editions, *III and XVII were included in a few as Ia and XIVa.